DEF. OF IQBALISM
P. 8

{ EXC. DEFINITION OF
FREE SPIRIT
PP. 86-87 }

FREE SPIRITS BATTLES
WITH SELF
P. 96

COMMUNITARIAN
INDIVIDUALISM
P. XXI

Nietzsche's
Noontide Friend

Literature & Philosophy

A. J. Cascardi, General Editor

This series publishes books in a wide range of subjects in philosophy and literature, including studies of the social and historical issues that relate these two fields. Drawing on the resources of the Anglo-American and Continental traditions, the series is open to philosophically informed scholarship covering the entire range of contemporary critical thought.

Already published:

Nietzsche's Noontide Friend

The Self
as
Metaphoric Double

Sheridan Hough

The Pennsylvania State University Press
University Park, Pennsylvania

Library of Congress Cataloging-in-Publication Data

Hough, Sheridan, 1961–
    Nietzsche's noontide friend : the self as metaphoric double /
Sheridan Hough.

        p.   cm. — (Literature & philosophy)
    Includes bibliographical references and index.
    ISBN 0-271-01649-3 (alk. paper)
    1. Nietzsche, Friedrich Wilhelm, 1844–1900.   2. Superman.   3. Self
(Philosophy)   4. Metaphor.   I. Title.   II. Series: Literature and
philosophy.
    B3318.S8H68   1997
    193 — dc20   96-38366
                                                                    CIP

It is the policy of The Pennsylvania State University Press to use acid-free paper for the
first printing of all clothbound books. Publications on uncoated stock satisfy the
minimum requirements of American National Standard for Information Sciences —
Permanence of Paper for Printed Library Materials, ANSI Z39.48-1992.

To
Vernon and Phyllis Hough

For a genuine poet, metaphor is not a rhetorical figure but a vicarious image that he actually beholds in place of a concept.
— *The Birth of Tragedy*, viii

Contents

Acknowledgments

In the preface to *Twilight of the Idols* Nietzsche remarks, "Nothing succeeds in which high spirits play no part." My work on this book has been the occasion for high-spirited play with some remarkable people.

When I began my graduate studies at Berkeley, I thought I would work on some topic in the philosophy of language, something reliable, safe, and far from the obscurity of existential philosophy. When I took Hubert Dreyfus's class on *Being and Time*, I realized that 'the question of Nietzsche' still plagued me, and that I wanted more than anything to give some shape to these 'obscurities'. This book bears the genetic stamp of its dissertation forbear, and I owe a debt to many of the philosophers I met and worked with during my time at Berkeley. First, I am grateful to Bert Dreyfus for teaching me how to approach Heidegger, and for encouraging me (in his generous and enthusiastic way) to find my own path through Nietzsche's texts. I hope that my rendition of Heidegger (in some respects now quite different from his own) is at least faithful to the spirit of his work. Bernard Williams has also been a great friend of this project. He read my doctoral work with care, and he pressed me to be both precise and daring. I thank him for sharing his prodigious interests and his sense of humor with me. My conversations with Donald Davidson about the philosophy of language played an important role in shaping my thoughts about this very different material (they were also great fun). Gregory Vlastos and Paul Feyerabend were both tremendously influential in my philosophical development, and I remember them as kind, generous, demanding, and wise.

Many colleagues, mentors, and friends have put up with me and my preoccupations over the years. Their intelligence and wit is visible throughout. Thanks to Curtis Brown, Michael DellaRocca, Katherine Eggert, Steven Luper, and Kayley Vernallis. Special thanks to Lawrence Kimmel for inspiring me to take up philosophy, and to Peter French for sharpening my abilities and telling me to carry on.

Much of this work was done while I was a Fellow of the Honors College at the University of Houston. Ted Estess, the dean of the college, arranged a semester's leave and a grant so that I could finish the book (which I did in marvelous solitude while living by a lake, with a blue heron for company). Cynthia Freeland encouraged me at the moments when I most needed it. Robert Zaretsky has been a special friend of this book, and so has Peter J. Potter of Penn State Press. My husband, Keith Fenech, has been at all times a loving and patient companion.

This work is about debt and inheritance, about the self as largely composed of cultural material that is shaped by a contingent process of socialization. Hence a person is, as Nietzsche would say, a piece of fate, the product of ineluctable fortune. It has been my incredible good fortune to be raised by the most loving of parents. Anything worthwhile in this account is the product of their intellectual curiosity, the joy they bring to their pursuits, their wisdom. This book is dedicated to them.

Preface

They are those true men, *those who are no longer animal,
the philosophers, artists, and saints;* nature . . . feels for the
first time it has reached its goal. . . . It is the fundamental
idea of culture, insofar as it sets for each one of us but one
task: *to promote the production of the philosopher, the artist,
and the saint within us and without us and thereby to work
at the perfecting of nature.* . . . Sometimes it is harder to
accede to a thing than it is to see its truth; and that is how
people may feel when they reflect on the proposition: 'Mankind must work continually on the production of individual
great men — that and nothing else is its task.'
          — Nietzsche, *Schopenhauer as Educator*

I

Who is this 'great individual'? Why is this person, in Nietzsche's estimation, the only appropriate goal of human life? If a person sets out to
accomplish Nietzsche's task, who would she or he become? Given that we
can adequately describe this individual, how do we go about 'reproducing'
his or her crucial features?

Certainly, such an individual would exhibit a wide range of great powers: the saintly strength of denial and discipline, the flexibility of the artist
and the philosopher's reflectiveness. Perhaps it is the allure of these
qualities that draws us to Nietzsche's exhortations and commandments.
No matter how we conceive of this elusive character, the sense of this
individual's activity, industry, and devotion remains palpable. Surely this
person is bursting with creativity and constantly absorbed in some endeavor.

As I searched for a description of this person in Nietzsche's texts, I discovered instead an individual quite different from this initial naïve rendering. With a perverse pleasure (surely the concomitant affect of every investigation of Nietzsche), I began to catalogue the ways in which this superior individual was also passive, self-effacing, ecstatic, and supremely receptive.

Nietzsche's account of the self has both 'active' and 'receptive' elements. The 'active' qualities are the usual objects of critical inquiry. For example, Nietzsche's 'free spirits' are highly reflective, intensely skeptical of the beliefs and practices of their culture, and calling these practices into question is their perspicuous 'activity'. I argue that this reflective activity is founded on a host of practices, largely unreflected upon, that in turn constitute the free spirits. Awareness of the self as a cultural product, as "a necessary chain of rings of culture,"[1] is an equally important dimension of Nietzsche's understanding of human nature, one that is often ignored by the traditional interest in Nietzsche's active dismantling (and indeed his praise of such dismantling) of these cultural values.

Heidegger's is perhaps the most important — certainly the most influential — of these traditional accounts. He has been a disturbing presence in my thinking about Nietzsche; this book is in many ways a response to Heidegger's claims about Nietzsche's 'metaphysics of value'. In his lectures on Nietzsche, Heidegger argues that a value is an articulation of a particular set of forces posited by the will to power: value is the 'voice' of will to power. These values are 'metaphysical' because they are the essential components of Being; human life is grounded in the creation and establishment of these values. The will to power marshals that set of values that can maintain and enhance it as a particular configuration of forces, so the criteria for choosing and promoting a particular value turn on its ability to sustain whatever form the will to power has currently adopted. No value can be preferred as such over any other, and the 'essence' of human existence turns out to be an incessant activity of taking up value in order to expand and promote the powers it makes available: one configuration of power is as worthwhile as the next. The person who sees this, and who is able to master this metaphysical machinery of the taking up and overcoming of value is, claims Heidegger, the Übermensch, the highest achievement of humanity.

Is this rather depressing account of human life really what Nietzsche proposes? I will return to this question in various ways, but my main claim

---

1. Nietzsche, *Human, All Too Human*, trans. R. J. Hollingdale (Cambridge: Cambridge University Press, 1986), 292.

is that this picture of the Übermensch, aggressively consuming and exploiting value, fails to accomodate the receptive side of Nietzsche's understanding of the human self (and, in particular, ignores the largely 'receptive' characterization of the Übermensch provided by Zarathustra).

The difference here is important. I argue that the person living what Nietzsche describes as the highest life understands and celebrates the narrow scope of human autonomy and our limited capacity to posit value. Heidegger's version of the Übermensch sees the world as a stockpile of values to be appropriated and mastered, an account that does not recognize the ways in which human beings are themselves constituted by these habits of life and thought. Heidegger claims that the most powerful activity in the Nietzschean economy is the overcoming of value; I claim that the most powerful moments in Nietzsche's texts are those that reveal how it is that members of a culture are shaped and created by value. Nietzsche remarks in *Daybreak* 552: "We . . . ought to blow to the wind all presumptuous talk of willing and creating." He urges us to acknowledge our debts, to see how much we owe to our language, our parenting, and our politics. Any act of 'overcoming' is indebted to forces that have made possible that act of positing and willing.

There are questions about the mechanism that Heidegger attributes to Nietzsche. How does the will to will posit value and overcome it? Is this activity essentially reflective, or largely carried out unreflectively, in practice? What is the nature of this positing?

I do not pursue any of these questions in this book because my objection to Heidegger's account is more fundamental. Regardless of how it is that the will to will posits and overcomes value, it is still the case that any account that places *will* as our essential activity does not question the source of the values so posited by will, nor can it acknowledge the ways in which the person positing value is *herself* constituted by value. Heidegger's understanding of Nietzsche revolves around an activity of will; my account focuses on the values that have already composed and determined that activity of willing.[2]

My critique of Heidegger's account of the Übermensch contains an obvious irony (although it is fitting that, in a book about doubleness, one of

---

2. The following passage from Heidegger's lectures on Nietzsche is paradigmatic: "The decisive question is this: do the willed and the one who wills belong to the willing of the will? Answer: on the grounds of willing and by means of willing. Willing wills the one who wills, as such a one; and willing posits the willed as such" (*Nietzsche: Volume One, The Will to Power as Art*, trans. and ed. David Farrell Krell [London: Routledge and Kegan Paul, 1981]).

the central figures should play two roles). As I struggled to structure my thoughts about Nietzschean 'receptivity', I found myself using Heidegger's own thoughts about the nature of the self. The 'existential analytic' of *Being and Time* schematizes the way in which 'human being' is always already constituted by its culture. Heidegger argues that the human essence is in effect no essence at all, but a capacity to embody a set of contingent practices. Heidegger emphatically places practice before theory. Our disinterested survey of the world and its contents is the detritus of a primordial oneness with the practical world. This practical activity should not be understood in terms of a subject engaged in an objective environment, but instead as an engagement constituted by a prior and nonmental connectedness.

Nietzsche's remarks about the 'receptive', culturally created self become much clearer using this Heideggerian lens of Being (perhaps this is what Foucault meant when he said that reading Nietzsche and Heidegger together was the 'great shock').[3] Heidegger's early work in *Being and Time* is central to my understanding of Nietzsche; but so too, I discovered, is some of Heidegger's later work. His analysis of 'world' versus 'earth' is a useful image of the tensions at work in Nietzsche's thinking. 'World' deliberates, articulates, calculates, while 'earth' is the recalcitrant and nonrationalizable source of these articulations. Nietzsche's descriptions of the artist, who simultaneously 'wills' her work while relying on inspiration, on a guiding vision, are strikingly similar to this struggle of 'world' and 'earth'.

Why are Heidegger's reflections on Being, both early and late, so Nietzschean in content (and, in the case of the later works, even in deployment) while Heidegger's explicit rendering of Nietzsche is so willfully (the pun is relevant) at odds with many of Nietzsche's claims? This is an intriguing question that must be raised elsewhere, (though, clearly, much would need to be said about Heidegger's use of Nietzsche's 'unthought').

Even though I disagree with Heidegger's official account of Nietzsche (namely, his provocative description of the Übermensch), his remarks have drawn my attention to the 'doubleness' of Nietzsche's thinking about the self. For every passage that praises he who 'commands' and 'wills', the careful reader of Nietzsche will always find a question mark: a person may will, but what is it (to paraphrase Deleuze) that wills in the person? We are more constituted than constituting, and our ability to critically examine, to

---

3. Michel Foucault, *Politics, Philosophy, Culture: Interviews and Other Writings, 1977–1984*, ed. Lawrence D. Kritzman (New York: Routledge, 1988), p. 250.

deliberate, to choose, lives in an uneasy alliance with a host of evaluations, practices, and habits that are at work on us and in us. Nietzsche does praise an activity of 'willing', but to focus an interpretation solely on this is to ignore the equally important presence of Nietzschean 'receptivity', the moments of 'grace' and inspiration, that are necessary for creative work to begin.

II

Doubleness is the central feature of Nietzsche's view of the self. A person is both a mind that wills and a creature that can be 'visited by a god' (more on this in Chapter 3). Avital Ronell calls this quality of Nietzsche's writings his 'rapport with the couple':

> Nietzsche's . . . alterity that is double or nothing — is indeed so strik-
> ing as to render Nietzsche the thinker par excellence of the couple:
> Lou and Paul, Dionysus and Apollo, Ariadne and Dionysus, Dionysus
> and the Antichrist, Wagner and Nietzsche, and what he becomes when
> he is: I am my mother and my father, *Ich bin der und der*.[4]

Nietzsche's most famous 'pair' is undoubtedly Apollo and Dionysos, a couple who offer a paradigm of Nietzsche's habitual conjoining of inter-twined qualities. In *The Birth of Tragedy*, Apollo and Dionysos personify two natural forms of human release, dreaming and intoxication. Nietzsche argues that the confluence of these somatic drives is art (and their highest union is the highest form of art, the tragedy). Apollo is emblematic of both mental and moral illumination, of the capacity to make distinctions and to organize concepts. Apollo individuates; that is, the clarity provided by Apollo gives ideas shape, our inchoate feelings become judgments. Diony-sos, as the god of the vine and the vitality of growing things, is a figure of untrammeled potency, the insistence and force of living things violently expressed.

What it is about the dream that is meant to be expressed by art? It is a mistake to think of the Apollinian as 'dreamy' or 'unreal'. What Nietzsche has in mind is the way in which a dream is a meaningful whole, a *cosmos*. Every element of the dream sphere is significant, and everything within

---

4. Avital Ronell, "Namely, Eckermann," in *Looking After Nietzsche*, ed. Laurence A. Rickels (New York: State University of New York Press, 1990), p. 235.

the dream is relevant, full of import and intent. Moreover, a dream is always a world a person sets before herself. The dream producer is the centerpiece of the dream, even if — or especially if — she does not appear in it. The terrors and delights of the dream are about, or for the benefit of, the dreamer: the dream is in that sense a way of highlighting the dreamer as a distinct individual.

The complement and mate of the dream impulse is intoxication. Narcotic self-dissolution shatters this sense of being discrete, separate, and whole (of course, drink is only one route to this kind of physical ecstasy).[5] Nietzsche identifies Dionysos as a god whose influence in other cultures is often wholly destructive;[6] what saved the Greeks from Dionysiac dismemberment, Nietzsche claims, was the presence of Apollinian tendencies. On the other hand, Dionysiac forces revealed a knowledge of suffering that the lyric beauty of Apollo denied. Each needed the other: "And behold! Apollo could not live without Dionysos."[7] The art that heals humankind is the offspring of these two forces;[8] accordingly, if we deny *either* impulse we destroy our capacity to save ourselves.

The most common misunderstanding of *The Birth of Tragedy* is that Nietzsche champions the Dionysian and denigrates the Apollinian, that he urges us to excise Socratism and the theoretical view (both degenerate ways of honoring the Apollinian) from human life. Even if we could make sense of this view — one that is wildly contradicted by the text — we can hardly find it plausible or desirable. Nietzsche does *not* object to the suppression of Dionysian forces by Apollinian clarity and order. In fact, he thinks that it is crucial: without the art that is generated by the forces of order and reason, we would be torn apart by our own viciousness, stupidity, greed, and lust. It is necessary and good to tame the forces that oppose individuation and order, but much depends on the way in which those forces are tamed. What will save us is art, and the highest art is jointly produced. In the final sentence of *The Birth of Tragedy* Nietzsche imagines Aeschylus exclaiming: "Now follow me to witness a tragedy, and sacrifice with me in the temple of both deities!"[9] Both tendencies must be nurtured and honored.

Though Nietzsche did not sustain *The Birth of Tragedy*'s view of the

---

5. Nietzsche, *The Birth of Tragedy*, trans. Walter Kaufmann (New York: Random House, 1967), section 1.

6. Nietzsche, *The Birth of Tragedy*, section 2.

7. Nietzsche, *The Birth of Tragedy*, section 4.

8. Ibid.

9. Nietzsche, *The Birth of Tragedy*, section 25.

redemptive power of art, Apollo and Dionysos are still paradigmatic of Nietzsche's characterization of the self, which is given in terms of opposed pairs of qualities and drives. He uses sets of metaphors to describe the human constitution, each metaphor needing to be understood in terms of its 'mate'. Nietzsche famously describes the self as composed of 'granite', but this granitic self is also self-investigating, by nature an archaeologist, driven to dig up the cultural tendencies of which he is made. Again, Nietzsche likens our ethical knowledge of ourselves to the 'land', and imagines a free-spirited launching out from the familiar and established into a 'sea' of critical reflection and interpretation. These explorers, the free spirits, have a peculiarly dual sense of themselves: as self-scrutinizing they are ever conscious of their 'shadow', yet they are occasionally rescued from this painful self-awareness by the ecstatic (and perfectly unshadowed) moment of 'noon'. Finally, Nietzsche diagnoses the free spirit's discordant sensibility (on the one hand, driven to overcome that which constitutes him; on the other, only escaping this imperative by lapsing into a narcotic stupor) with the metaphoric pair of 'pregnancy' and the 'child at play'. These images are Nietzsche's oblique account of a healthy and productive autonomy.

Each of these pairs of metaphors has an 'active' and 'receptive' element. As with Apollo and Dionysos, one half structures, creates, and establishes, while the other half disrupts, dissolves, and commingles. I found it difficult to keep both accounts — the description of a receiving self and that of an active, creative self — in clear view. It is always tempting to describe only one of the 'faces' Nietzsche offers us (although he himself reminds us in *Ecce Homo* that all great perceptions are 'Janus-faced').[10] However, it became clear to me that many useful critical accounts of Nietzsche lose sight of one or the other half of the pair in question at precisely the moment in which sensitivity to its subterranean presence is most needed. Nietzsche is committed to providing oppositions that are not 'opposed', that can only be fruitfully understood as an interpretive unit. Any commentary on Nietzsche ignores this truth at its peril.[11]

---

10. Nietzsche, "Human, All Too Human," in *Ecce Homo*, trans. R. J. Hollingdale (New York: Penguin Books, 1979), section 6.

11. I should sound a cautionary note about the labels 'active' and 'receptive', which inevitably suggest Deleuze's famous pairing of activity and reactivity (*Nietzsche et la philosophie* [Paris: Presses Universitaires de France, 1962]). 'Activity/receptivity' is not the same sort of opposition, the most obvious reason being that ultimately these qualities are meant (somehow) to combine: The ideal life is at the same time both of these things. 'Activity/reactivity' are forces truly opposed to one another. 'Reactivity' is actually a force, although a descending one; it makes assertions and stakes claims just as activity does. The

III

> Let us take . . . the astonishing stroke of Hegel, who struck
> right through all our logical habits and bad habits when he
> dared to teach that species concepts (die Artbegriffe) develop
> *out of each other*.
>
> — *The Gay Science* 357

Nietzsche's philosophical produce was grown in Hegelian soil. Any adequate unearthing of Nietzsche's thinking (to use his own persistent epistemic metaphor) will uncover many of Hegel's intellectual concerns and tendencies, a few of which I will mention here.

I will not, here or elsewhere in this book, assess Nietzsche's attack on Hegel.[12] With Nietzschean polemics context is everything, and Hegel is often deliberately misrepresented by Nietzsche in order to achieve more immediate rhetorical ends.[13] The following remarks have to do with Nietzsche's Hegelian inheritance, and with the genetic connection between Hegel's grand *geistig* system and Nietzsche's nonsystematic aphorisms and images.

Several shared concerns immediately come to mind. First, and most generally, my portrait of Nietzsche as a thinker of opposed terms (oppositions that are only fully understood and indeed realized in interrelation to one another) is a perfectly adequate (if generic) description of Hegel's own phenomenology. More specifically, Hegel's description of the unhappy consciousness (self-consciousness that is driven both to recognize and to denounce its material nature vis-à-vis the realm of pure spirit) is given an elaborate and highly specific reading by Nietzsche in *The Genealogy of Morals* as the work of *ressentiment* and the ascetic ideal.[14] Both philosophers want to repudiate the metaphysical conceit of the 'real' versus the

---

problem with reactivity is the way in which its claims are made, namely, through sublimation and displacement. My notion of 'receptivity' is in no way a perversion of the powers employed in activity, but rather its necessary completion.

12. Cf. Gilles Deleuze's discussion of Nietzsche's view of Hegel in *Nietzsche et la philosophie*.

13. Some of these are irresistably funny. For example, his assault on German culture in *Daybreak* 190 indicts Schiller, Schleiermacher, and von Humboldt as well as Hegel: "What is it in them that seems to us, as we are today, now so insupportable, so pitiable and moving? First, their thirst for appearing morally excited at any cost; then, their desire for brilliant, boneless generalities."

14. See M. Greene's "Hegel's 'Unhappy Consciousness' and Nietzsche's 'Slave Morality'," in *Hegel and the Philosophy of Religion*, ed. D. Christensen (The Hague: Martinus Nijhoff, 1970), 125–41.

'apparent' world, and to supplant such dualisms with a holistic and vital characterization of the world.[15] Hegel famously proposes *Sittlichkeit*, the ethical life, as the proper dialectical goal of individual development. He argues that human fulfillment is possible only within a communal context. Nietzsche is also struck by the importance of cultural membership, although his worry about self-realization is different from Hegel's. Nietzsche sees us as cultural products, and the slogan 'wie man wird, was man ist' has everything to do with coming to terms with that cultural make-up, as individuals and as members of a community. This is not the kind of culmination that Hegel envisions, namely, the individual as a participant in the evolution of justice and reason. The Nietzschean sense in which a person reaches a kind of maturity by taking stock of her cultural 'structure' *HIS* is the subject of Chapter 3.

The most potent resemblance, however, between Hegel and Nietzsche (and one that has guided my reading of Nietzsche) has to do with what we might call the temper of their work, that of *Bewegung*, 'movement'. Both Hegel and Nietzsche want to capture the dynamic character of life itself. The assertions made by Hegel in his speculative metaphysics depend on this dynamism: it is never a question of *A* being corrected by *B*, but how it is that *B* is the dialectical product of *A*. Hegel remarks in the Preface of the *Phenomenology of Spirit*:

> The more conventional opinion gets fixated on the antithesis of truth and falsity. . . . It does not comprehend the diversity of philosophical systems as the progressive unfolding of truth, but rather sees in it simple disagreements. The bud disappears in the bursting-forth of the blossom, and one might say that the former is refuted by the latter; similarly, when the fruit appears, the blossom is shown up in its turn as a false manifestation of the plant, and the fruit now emerges as the truth of it instead. These forms are not just distinguished from one another, they also supplant one another as mutually incompatible. Yet at the same time their fluid nature makes them moments of an organic unity in which they not only do not conflict, but in which each is as

---

15. See Daniel Breazeale, "The Hegel-Nietzsche Problem," *Nietzsche-Studien* 4 (1975): 146–64; and Stephen Houlgate, *Hegel, Nietzsche and the Criticism of Metaphysics* (Cambridge: Cambridge University Press, 1986). Houlgate's account of Hegel in this work is remarkable, but the comparison with Nietzsche is flawed by the presence of some standard interpretive assumptions: Houlgate characterizes Nietzsche as devaluing communal identity and championing autonomy in the guise of individual creativity and growth. He claims that Nietzsche presents the will to power as the one basic reality. This book questions all of these claims.

necessary as the other; and this mutual necessity alone constitutes the life of the whole.[16]

In order to have an adequate understanding of Hegel's project, the dynamic quality of his claims must be acknowledged. Hegel's speculative metaphysics should not be read as a set of assertions;[17] rather, he would have us see that the dialectical *movement* inherent in our claims (and in life itself) is the context within which what we aver makes sense. So too with Nietzsche (and perhaps in his case the ability to sense this is even more imperative). Nietzsche's hyperbolic accusations and claims must be understood in terms of his larger philosophical intent, namely, to describe our moral, intellectual, and spiritual natures as a *process* endured rather than as a state attained. Nietzsche's avowals have many local, specific uses; they can shock, offend, delight, mislead, even lie. I argue that each of these declarations must be interpreted in terms of a larger tropic network that is built on tension, difference, complement, and *the movement between* opposing claims.[18]

And here, of course, is where the Nietzschean flower eclipses the Hegelian bud. Nietzsche's vigorous depiction of human thought and life has no taint of Hegelian teleology. Hegel describes the movement of *Geist* in history as a succession of stages unfolding by virtue of an immanent goal. He regards human endeavor as cumulative and progressive. This developmental story also justifies the suffering and calamity that are a necessary part of this historical progress. Nietzsche denies this redemptive tale. His own version of 'redemption', the eternal return of the same, offers us necessity without an accompanying higher or greater sense: we are invited to will that every accident and misfortune (as well as every triumph) recur infinitely, without alteration. The possibility of interpreting the vicissitudes of human life in evolutionary terms is rejected. I will say more about what it might mean to will the eternal return in Chapter 3.

---

16. G. W. F. Hegel, *The Phenomenology of Spirit*, trans. A.V. Miller (Oxford: Oxford University Press, 1977), p. 2.

17. Houlgate provides an illuminating discussion of this in chapter 5 of his *Hegel, Nietzsche, and the Criticism of Metaphysics*.

18. Both Hegel and Nietzsche use the notion of play or sport to describe this dynamism. In the *Phenomenology* Hegel remarks: "Thus the life of God and divine cognition may well be spoken of as a disporting of Love within itself [*ein Spielen der Liebe mit sich selbst*]; but this idea sinks into . . . insipidity if it lacks the seriousness, the suffering, the patience, and the labor of the negative"; that is, the hard work of the dialectician, who fully characterizes this *Spielen* (p. 10). Of course, "dem Spiele des Schaffens," the sport of creation, is the chief occupation of the child of "den drei Verwandlungen."

Futhermore, the 'doubleness' of Nietzsche's metaphors, the fruitful tension and dynamic contradiction in which they stand, is not synthetic in Hegel's terms. These oppositions do not evolve via a series of determinate negations into higher concepts or greater self-understanding. They do generate new ideas and new forms of life, but not in a progressive or determinate fashion. More important, 'progress' and even 'new forms of life' are wholly beside the point for Nietzsche, and that is why he is committed to the decidedly incomplete metaphor of pregnancy as his emblem of the highest life (the subject of Chapter 4).

IV

Who, then, is this person that Nietzsche imagines in the third essay of his *Untimely Meditations?* My task in this book is to describe Nietzsche's account of the self and the ways in which he conceives of human potential being supremely realized. There is a preliminary clue in the model of the 'saint, artist, philosopher': all three share a particular kind of experience, which we might call the eclipse of the will, the will in the grip of a vision, an idea, a beautiful form that demands to be realized. All three are necessarily receptive to forces beyond their immediate reckoning, and this makes them, in a sense, inscrutable. They can communicate their embryonic sensibility only through a productive act, by bringing forth a treatise, a painting, a holy deed. In many cases, the results of their creative labors are unexpected — perhaps not even immediately recognizable. This person will thus necessarily be an active creator *as well as* a sensitive interpreter of the cultural materials that constitute her. She will be actively concerned with her cultural practices while supremely receptive to her own deepest sensibilities and atavisms. She will press for change while accepting that change is not always possible. She will scrutinize everyone and everything, yet she will also insist that reflection has its limits and misapplications. Finally, she will recognize that the best form of 'yea-saying' is not an articulation at all, but a moment of joy.

This person is not explicitly characterized in Nietzsche's writings (and never, as I have done, with the feminine pronoun); rather, this person comes into focus through the double vision of metaphor pairs. Rendering a metaphor is always a dubious undertaking and not to be thought of as giving its 'meaning'. To ask what these metaphors 'mean' is misguided. Donald Davidson remarks that this question is like asking how many facts or propositions are provided in a photograph: "None, an infinity, or one great unstable fact?"[19] Davidson goes on to say that although a metaphor can only mean what it literally says, it is worthwhile to investigate the *effect* of a metaphor, and to think about what it is that it brings to our attention. That is what I attempt in this book: an analysis of Nietzsche's systematic use of specific metaphors, and what those images direct us toward. My analysis does not, for the most part, use the psycholanalytic or poststructuralist methods that are often brought to bear on Nietzsche's images, although I will remark on some of their conclusions. Nor will I be writing in metaphor as, for example, Luce Irigaray does in *Amante Marine*. I have struggled to retain the vividness of Nietzsche's prose while focusing on his implicit concepts and arguments. Sarah Kofman, with some sympathy, offers this advice on the problem: "It seems to me more Nietzschean to write conceptually in the knowledge that a concept has no greater value than a metaphor and is itself a condensate of metaphors . . . than to write metaphorically while denigrating the concept."[20] Working with metaphor is philosophically daunting, but Nietzsche himself seems to think that such work is good exercise; he calls the deciphering of metaphor 'proof of the strong spirit'.[21] My discussion is at least, I hope, the occasion for such exercise.

My approach to these metaphor pairs is as follows: Chapter 1 begins with a discussion of Nietzsche's view of the self, composed of cultural 'granite', yet driven to 'archaeology', to an unearthing of those cultural materials. Nietzsche claims that no metaphysical model of the self obtains, and he emphasizes a kind of creative behavior in which a person 'wills' the kind of person he or she becomes. However, Nietzsche also remarks on the 'fated' quality of a person's character. Familial, educational, and cultural forces come together in shaping an individual, and that inheritance, although not 'metaphysical', is nonetheless 'foundational'. I conclude that a person's creative activity is not therefore a series of arbitrary interests or creative 'whims', but an investigation of this 'inheritance', which is not *itself* created or willed.

Chapter 2 explores how this 'foundation' may be useful in explaining what Nietzsche means by 'perspective'. Perspectives can be understood in

19. Donald Davidson, "What Metaphors Mean," in *On Metaphor*, ed. Sheldon Sacks (Chicago: University of Chicago Press, 1979), p. 45.

20. Sarah Kofman, *Nietzsche and Metaphor*, trans. Duncan Large (Stanford: Stanford University Press, 1983), p. 3.

21. Nietzsche, "Ancient Rhetoric," in *Friedrich Nietzsche on Rhetoric and Language*, trans. Sander Gilman, Carole Blair, and David Parent (Oxford: Oxford University Press, 1989), p. 55.

both an 'active' and a 'receptive' sense: a person's 'active' behavior is his or her reflective, representational behavior. For example, in taking up different points of view, such as the point of view of a culture or a discipline, a person takes up a different 'perspective'. This sort of perspective, however, is quite different from what I call a person's 'embodied' perspective. This receptive sense of 'perspective' has to do with the inherited practices and capacities that make up a person's view of the world. Unlike the simpler notion of 'foundation', however, an embodied perspective is not something that can be absolutely identified or described. A person is always engaged in the interpretive activity of understanding his embodied perspective; no final account can be given. When Nietzsche describes the 'land' we inhabit, he is pointing out this cultural 'ground' we share, and the image of being at sea, of going to sea, is a remark about the shifting perspectives that emerge when our common ground is displaced by reflection.

Chapter 3 discusses Nietzsche's psychological account of this reflective acitivity. The free spirit is dogged by a shadow, a shadow cast by the free spirit's efforts to overcome himself. Perfect noon is the moment of ecstatic release for the free spirit, the instant when all shadows are themselves overcome. I will claim that the metaphors of 'noon' and 'shadow' help us to identify the free spirit and the Übermensch, the 'active' and 'receptive' actors in Zarathustra's drama. The free spirit is relentlessly critical, but this activity is balanced by the presence of the Übermensch. Rather than seeing the Übermensch as a separate, 'superhuman' entity, I argue that the Übermensch is an ecstatic moment (Augenblick) in the experience of the free spirit. This moment of supreme blessing and self-acceptance is also a supremely receptive moment.

Finally, I claim that the ubiquitous image of pregnancy in Nietzsche's writings is Nietzsche's metaphor for the ideal individual and the ideal life. First, gestation is importantly ambiguous: is the pregnant woman one entity, or two? Is she pregnant *in order to* have the child, or is the pregnancy itself a kind of celebration of being human? By using passages from Plato's *Symposium* and *Phaedrus*, I maintain that Nietzsche's devotion to this metaphor rests on this important ambiguity. Nietzsche is challenging our sense of autonomy, and calling into question the absolute authority of reason. The trope of spiritual pregnancy indicates that a great individual will take up ideas, practices, and projects in order to effect change, to raise questions and propose new answers. However, that person will also be simultaneously celebrating his or her strengths and powers in a way that is wholly noninstrumental.

1

Ontology

the 'granite stratum' and its 'archaeology'

What is this earth that it attains to the unconcealed in just
such a manner?

—Heidegger, *The Origin of the Work of Art*

How can Nietzsche, shrill advo-
cate of creation and self-invention, claim that a person's nature is largely
fixed? We are, as he remarks, not only 'firm and settled', but a 'great stupidity':

> Learning transforms us, it does that which all nourishment does which
> does not merely 'preserve' —: as the physiologist knows. But at the
> bottom of us, 'right down deep', there is, to be sure, something un-
> teachable, a granite stratum of spiritual fate, of predetermined deci-
> sion and answer to predetermined selected questions. In the case of
> every cardinal problem there speaks an unchangeable 'this is I': about
> man and woman, for example, a thinker cannot relearn but only learn
> fully — only discover all that is 'firm and settled' within him on this
> subject. One sometimes comes upon certain solutions to problems
> which inspire strong belief in *us*; perhaps one thenceforth calls
> them convictions. Later—one sees them only as footsteps to self-
> knowledge, signposts to the problem which we are — more correctly,
> to the great stupidity which we are, to our spiritual fate, to the unteach-
> able 'right down deep'. — Having just paid myself such a deal of pretty
> compliments I may perhaps be more readily permitted to utter a few
> truths about 'woman as such': assuming it is now understood from the
> outset to how great an extent these are only — *my* truths. —

My investigation of metaphor begins with the famous section 231 of
Beyond Good and Evil. The passage is in fact prefigured in many of

Nietzsche's early writings, such as section 223 in *Assorted Opinions and Maxims*, the second volume of *Human, All Too Human*:

> The last three centuries very probably still continue to live on, in all their cultural colors and cultural refractions, close beside us: they want only to be discovered. In many families, indeed in individual men, the strata still lie neatly and clearly one on top of the other: elsewhere there are dislocations and faults which make the understanding more difficult.

And this remark from the third *Untimely Meditation*, "Schopenhauer as Educator":

> Your true educators and formative teachers reveal to you what the true basic material of your being is, *something in itself ineducable and in any case difficult of access*, bound and paralysed: your educators can be only your liberators.[1]

These depictions of Nietzschean 'character', its profundity and 'solidity' as well as its 'stupidity', are troubling. They suggest that the structure and nature of character is discovered rather than altered, given rather than invented. How can this be? How can the herald and harbinger of the free-spirited re-valuation of value believe that we are largely incapable of reinventing ourselves?

Questions about character immediately invite thoughts about Nietzsche's assault on morality. Certainly, Nietzsche's account of the free spirit's attack on prevailing moral norms will look very different if we have doubts about the extent to which the free spirits have actually managed to divest themselves of those views. The passages just quoted suggest a person who can do no more than find out what is central to her sense of the world: but not, it seems, radically reshape that sense. I shall explain what this 'granitic' metaphor has to say about the formation of character, and ethical concerns will of course play a role in this developmental story. In laying out Nietzsche's metaphoric model of the self (indeed, anti-model), I start by considering Nietzsche's critique of ethics, noting the kind of imperatives that may be generated by his understanding of the human constitution.

In *Daybreak* Nietzsche claims that his own recognition of the 'granite

---

1. Nietzsche, "Schopenhauer as Educator," *Untimely Meditations*, trans. R. J. Hollingdale (Cambridge: Cambridge University Press, 1983), section 1.

stratum' created a personal imperative: he was compelled to become an 'archaeologist', a complex and obscure undertaking that needs to be distinguished from what might ordinarily be called becoming a 'cultural historian' or perhaps 'cultural psychologist'. This metaphorical pair, the strata of human nature that invite excavation, suggests Foucault's own use of the archaeological trope.

I

The 'granitic' account is a curious and difficult place to begin investigating Nietzsche's account of the self, since it stands in an uncertain, perhaps contradictory, relation to the most familiar of Nietzsche's views about human nature: his well-known and much discussed anti-essentialism. Nietzsche's opposition to any account that appeals to metaphysical grounds is the starting point of a whole range of inquiries, and it is regularly appealed to (in multifarious and sometimes questionable ways) by many who write and think in the deconstructionist tradition. Generally, Nietzsche's 'anti-essentialism' involves questions about the status of our knowledge claims: to what do such claims attempt to appeal, if not to the 'absolute nature' of things? More narrowly, Nietzsche is interested in the status of claims about our nature: can we say anything definitive about the human constitution, and in turn, anything definitive about how we should live? A staggering amount of recent criticism (particularly concerning Foucault) makes use of Nietzschean antimetaphysics (in fact, that label, 'Nietzsche's denial of metaphysics', is the usual formula in these works) without specifying exactly what part of Nietzsche's assault on metaphysics is involved. This so-called denial is forced to do a lot of backstage work in these accounts, sometimes filling in the gaps in a schematic argument on the lines of "we can dismiss x because we have, in Nietzsche's phrase, 'overcome' metaphysics."

No doubt the 'essentials' of Nietzsche's anti-essentialist account of human nature, thus described, are obvious; nevertheless, some of the claims advanced in the name of Nietzsche show an equally obvious insensitivity to his favorite metaphor of the self. If the 'self' is utterly without boundaries, completely fluid, self-interpreting, self-creating, as many readers of Nietzsche conclude, then why does Nietzsche consistently describe human nature as the accreted and scarcely mobile muck of the ages? If the self has no foundation, no ground, then why does he describe human nature as literally a plot of 'ground'? The implications of this metaphor must be taken seriously, and must be brought to bear on his more familiar accounts of the self as creative and self-interpreting.[2] A closer look at Nietzsche's anti-essentialism is called for.

Nietzsche's skepticism about 'essentialism' exists on two levels. First, he doubts any foundational claim about human beings as such (for example, "Man is essentially a rational animal"). Second, he doubts claims about particular individuals (such as "Fred is an essentially bitter person"). Any history, whether natural or personal, is open to revision. This claim may seem completely unacceptable; how, then, can Nietzsche say anything about human behavior at all? Indeed, Nietzsche undermines virtually every standard model of the self.

> The 'inner world' is full of phantoms and false lights: the will is one of them. The will no longer moves anything, consequently it no longer explains anything—it merely accompanies events. . . . And as for the ego! It has become a fable, a fiction, a play on words.[3]

> The 'subject' is not something given, it is something added and invented and projected behind what there is.[4]

> Truly, the individual himself is still the most recent creation.[5]

> The concepts 'individual' and 'species' [are] equally false and merely apparent. 'Species' expresses only the fact that an abundance of similar creatures appear at the same time . . . the form counts as something enduring and therefore more valuable; but the form has merely been invented by us; and however often 'the same form is attained', it does not mean that it is the same form—what appears is always something new.[6]

If 'subject', 'ego', 'will', and 'species' are convenient fictions, what in fact is Nietzsche talking about when he discusses human nature? What about

---

2. Cf. Carol Gilligan's shrewd remark: "To speak of the body as text is one thing. To suggest that this writing and re-writing is happening on something other than on a blank slate or screen is to court the demon essentialism" (*London Review of Books* [July 1993]).

3. Nietzsche, "The Four Great Errors," in *Twilight of the Idols*, trans. R. J. Hollingdale (New York: Penguin Books, 1968), p. 3.

4. Nietzsche, *The Will To Power*, trans. Walter Kaufmann (New York: Vintage Books, 1968), p. 481. See References for my comments on the use of these portions of the *Nachlass*.

5. Nietzsche, "The Thousand and One Goals," in *Thus Spoke Zarathustra*, Part 1, trans. R. J. Hollingdale (New York: Penguin Books, 1961).

6. Nietzsche, *The Will to Power* 521.

those human qualities that he so tirelessly criticizes, such as vanity: why does 'vanity' not form part of the human constitution? When Nietzsche calls vanity the "human 'thing in itself' " and remarks that vanity is the thing "most vulnerable and yet the most unconquerable,"[7] what does he mean?

The familiar comment that Nietzsche denies any notion of 'human nature' seems strange when one reviews the myriad, highly detailed descriptions he gives of it. Nonetheless, these descriptions are provisional and contingent: Nietzsche usually qualifies his acceptance of these descriptions by (apparently) contradicting himself in a later passage or by simply telling us that his views are temporary and subject to revision. Nietzsche's infamous treatment of women provides an excellent example of such qualification. Witness the following passage from *Human, All Too Human*:

> Can women be just at all if they are so used to loving, to feeling immediately pro or con? For this reason they are also less often partial to causes, more often to people; but if to a cause, they immediately become partisan, therefore ruining its pure, innocent effect . . . what would be more rare than a woman who really knew what science is? The best even nourish in their hearts a secret disdain for it, as if they were somehow superior.
> *Perhaps all this can change; for the time being it is so.*[8]

But for the final sentence, Nietzsche would have us believe that his characterization of women reveals what women essentially *are*, rather than what they have become through an extensive history of socialization. Nine sections later Nietzsche clarifies this difference:

> *Women's period of storm and stress*. In the three or four civilized European countries, *one can in a few centuries educate women to be anything one wants, even men* — not in the sexual sense, of course, but certainly in every other sense. At some point, under such an influence, they will have taken on all male virtues and strengths, and of course they will also have to take male weakness and vice into the bargain.[9]

7. Nietzsche, *Assorted Opinions and Maxims*, trans. R. J. Hollingdale (Cambridge: Cambridge University Press, 1986), p. 46. See References: *Menschliches, Allzumenschliches*.

8. Nietzsche, *Human, All Too Human* 416; emphasis mine.

9. Ibid., 425; emphasis mine.

Now we are faced with several levels of description: what women are presently like, what women can come to be like, and what women are essentially. The implication is that there is some hidden 'chameleon quality' that allows women (and presumably men as well) to create new characteristics and features that may even contradict previously existing characteristics and features. Is this 'chameleon quality' the nature that we should be investigating, or is it also merely a provisional description?

Heidegger's Dasein is an excellent — and, again, familiar — propaedeutic to sorting out these questions because Dasein is an explicit rendering of this suggestive indeterminacy. As I said in the Preface, it is ironic that my explanation of Nietzsche should use some of Heidegger's central views on the structure of the self (from both his early and later works), since ultimately I will call into question Heidegger's explicit rendering of Nietzsche. Nevertheless, if we set aside the question of how much the existential analytic of *Being and Time* owes to Nietzsche (and why this influence goes unacknowledged), we can appreciate the clarity that the structure of Dasein brings to Nietzsche's unstructured and lyrical account of the self.

To begin with an uncontroversial comparison: Dasein, like the women Nietzsche describes, may also be crudely characterized as having a 'chameleon quality', although this kind of mutability never shows up at the level of the individual. Individual Dasein is not a positing, subjective 'I' within an objective world, but is, we might say, already part of a world of sharing practices and coping strategies. Individuals are always already an instance of a set of cultural skills and practices, namely, the 'background' against which and within which the individual understands himself and the world. Dasein as a phenomenon 'is what it does', and the scope of available practices is determined by its self-interpretive structure.[10]

These 'understandings of Being', these 'self-interpretations' that constitute Dasein are not understandings or interpretations in the sense in which the existential analytic is an understanding or an interpretation; an under-

---

10. Here we should issue a caveat about certain unavoidable expressions that create difficulties in any discussion of *Being and Time*. Indeed, the remark that "Dasein is what it interprets itself to be" does *not* mean that a person reflectively works out an understanding of herself that she therefore becomes; it is this sort of subjective idealism that Heidegger is intent on denying. In order to characterize Heidegger's remarks adequately, we must first distinguish between a kind of philosophical endeavor, such as Heidegger's, and the everyday sort of self-examination that is patently unphilosophical. Heidegger's undertaking, the existential analytic, is (obviously) an explicit, reflective pursuit, which draws an ontological conclusion, namely, that 'human being' is essentially the capacity to take up various interpretations of what it is to be human. Human beings 'become' a variety of interpretations over time.

standing of Being is not reflective, consciously chosen, or explicit.[11] Furthermore, a person is always *already composed* of various social practices and norms. Her carriage, temperament, the way she handles objects around her (such as tools, or furniture) — indeed, the very objects around her — are 'pieces' of that 'understanding of Being'. This 'understanding' is thus largely (in fact, in some cases utterly) *not* available for conscious scrutiny at all.

The remark that Dasein 'takes a stand' on its own being does not mean that every human being — or even most — engages in, for example, philosophical ontology: it means instead that human lives have an *implicit* understanding of Being, and exhibit an implicit interpretation of what it is to be human. Human being is essentially and implicitly self-interpreting; it is essentially no one interpretation, but the potential to embody an interpretation.

Although much more could be said of Heidegger's existential account, the following summation is adequate for our comparison: the 'understanding' and 'interpretation' displayed by Dasein are to be heard as nonreflective, nonexplicit embodiments of practices and norms. Subjectivism, or the claim that a person reflectively constructs and consciously inhabits a self — the notion that a person just is whatever she thinks she is — is not the being of Dasein. On the contrary, Heidegger's view implies that what persons truly are (both culturally and ontologically) the interpretation and existential structure implicit in their behavior, is mostly hidden from them: the person 'sees through it', and focuses on concerns that their implicit cultural interpretation has generated.

Heidegger claims that his formal designation of human being undermines all other metaphysical descriptions. Any metaphysical description falls within its boundaries. If we claim that human beings are, to consult Hubert Dreyfus's list, essentially 'rational animals', or essentially 'children of God', or essentially 'thinking machines', we have each time done the same thing, provided an understanding of ourselves, for ourselves.[12] In this respect these accounts are interchangeable; the content may be different but each gives us an understanding of ourselves, which is what we

---

11. Heidegger remarks, "With the term understanding . . . we have in mind . . . neither a definite species of cognition distinguished, let us say, from explaining or conceiving, nor any cognition at all in the sense of grasping something thematically" (Heidegger, *Being and Time*, trans. John Macquarrie and Edward Robinson [New York: Harper and Row, 1962]), p. 385.

12. Hubert Dreyfus, *Being-in-the-World: A Commentary on Heidegger's Being and Time, Division I* (Cambridge: MIT Press, 1991), p. 24.

are always giving, since this is what Dasein does. No particular account is right, but each one reveals us as self-interpreting beings.

Heidegger's existential analytic also denies that we as a species have something identifiable as 'human nature'. The designation 'Dasein' does not tell us what human beings are like, but gives us only a formal definition of what it is that human beings do. To say that human creatures take a stand on who they are says nothing about the scope and variety of these stands, nor does it provide us with a way to 'rank' these interpretive stances, or to prefer one cultural understanding to another.

To use another example: human beings are either male or female, but this fact is never 'bare', for it must always exist in a cultural context, in which 'masculine' and 'feminine' have already been given specific significance. Now we may fruitfully return to Nietzsche's remark about what women can become: "One can in a few centuries educate women to be anything one wants, even men — not in the sexual sense, of course, but certainly in every other sense." A person's physical sex constitutes a kind of natural boundary on what one can become through cultural evolution.[13] Nietzsche does not make the idealist claim that the way we see ourselves determines what we are. The material provided by nature, however, is too thin to determine any one way of understanding it, and so males and females become the historical hosts for many attributes, not all of which (perhaps none of which) can be true of them at all times: for example, men are active, men are mentally and morally superior; women are nurturing, women are essentially passive. Nietzsche himself makes a sizeable (and remarkably offensive) contribution to the category of female attributes. Fortunately, Nietzsche seems to believe that these characteristics are contingent, historical, and changeable: human beings can reinterpret themselves. Women can emulate the empowered sex by adopting their attire, body postures, and so forth, until they too comport themselves in business and society as 'men'. Since the essential female nature is a 'fiction', women — and men — can alter their traditional identity, perhaps indefinitely.

Nietzsche also says that this transformation is only possible 'in three or four civilized European countries', which sounds as if not all women are able to transform themselves. This inability is historical, not 'essential'. Only three or four European countries, at the time of Nietzsche's writing, were skeptical enough of their self-understanding for such a transforma-

---

13. *Human, All Too Human* 416. Athough in the case of hermaphrodites and sex changes, for example, the natural boundary is itself under dispute.

tion to take place. The traditions that had formerly constituted their society were being called into question. Obviously, the more 'traditional' a society is, and the more closely people identify with the kind of interpretations assigned to them by the culture, the less chance there is that anyone will ask why women are thought to be not as capable (for instance) as men. Nietzsche makes a comparable observation in the passage that began this chapter, *Assorted Opinions and Maxims* 223.

> A venerable specimen of very much older sensibility could certainly have been more easily preserved in remoter regions, in less travelled mountain valleys, in more self-enclosed communities: while it is improbable that such discoveries would be made in, for example, Berlin, where people come into the world washed and scalded clean.

A postmodern version of this tale is the easy and fashionable discourse about gender as construct that must occasionally confront, in places removed from university culture, the as yet largely unquestioned idea that men and women have distinct and biologically destined natures.

Nietzsche's remarks are, to say the least, deployed differently from Heidegger's.[14] Obviously, Nietzsche is not committed to a structural account, as Heidegger is. Nietzsche does not describe a revealing mood such as anxiety,[15] nor does he provide any formal assertions about human beings that are comparable to the existential analytic. Like Heidegger, however, Nietzsche is clearly skeptical about any absolute (namely, metaphysical) account of a person. As we have seen, Nietzsche heaps scorn on virtually *every* model of the self: the 'subject', the 'ego', the 'soul', the 'individual', and even the (reified) 'will' are all called into question. But in saying that no subject, ego, soul, individual, or will exists, what has Nietzsche actually denied? Or, more directly, what is it in a person that is 'left over' to which we may attribute characteristics? Let us recall that Nietzsche makes concrete claims about an individual's character. We can now return to his most familiar metaphor of the self and call such claims

---

14. This difference is more than a matter of 'deployment'; indeed, Nietzsche's rapturous, metaphoric style is hardly comparable to Heideggerian pedagogy. Nietzsche is clearly addressing the same sorts of concerns as Heidegger, albeit in a far less 'straightforward' manner. The impact of Nietzsche's style, and the kind of conclusion his approach to these questions provides, is something we ultimately should consider.

15. He does not often describe moments of insight in terms of fear or terror; for example, the demon's thought experiment, the Madman's assertions, Zarathustra's nightmares. Of course, Heideggerian 'anxiety' bears only a superficial relation to emotional unsettledness and fear.

'granitic' in their assurances. But how does this 'granite stratum' and 'unchangeable "this is I"' differ from the accounts of the self that Nietzsche denies? How do we reconcile Nietzsche's claim that a person's character has a 'granite' foundation with his claim that it has no foundation? Why does a person's 'spiritual granite' not serve as what we would identify as the 'subject', the 'individual', the essential grounding for that person's character?

A passage from *Human, All Too Human* indicates a way out of this difficulty. In the section entitled "On the History Of the Moral Sensations," Nietzsche remarks:

> *The unalterable character.* — In the strict sense, it is not true that one's character is unchangeable; rather, this popular tenet means only that during a man's short lifetime the motives affecting him cannot normally cut deep enough to destroy the imprinted writing of many millennia. If a man eighty thousand years old were conceivable, his character would in fact be absolutely variable, so that out of him little by little an abundance of different individuals would develop. The brevity of human life misleads us to many an erroneous assertion about the qualities of man.[16]

Here we have a model for thinking about the 'granite aspect' of our personalities. A person grows up in, and is shaped by, her parenting, her education, her genetic inheritance, her location in the prevailing class structure, and so forth: "the imprinted writing of many millennia." Many of the attitudes that shape a lifetime are formed long before one is able to articulate and 'own' those attitudes; for example, if a baby is surrounded by books of all manner, if her parents read to her and give her books to play with, she will most likely grow up feeling comfortable with books, and liking books.[17] However, we might also tell a less happy story. Suppose this female baby absorbs the notion that women should be thin, in fact, the thinner the better. This baby reaches maturity with food as 'the enemy'; she repeatedly starves herself, and punishes herself if she eats what might be considered by others as a normal amount of food. Perhaps one of her colleagues notices her behavior and implores her to get counseling or join

---

16. Nietzsche, *Human, All Too Human* 41.

17. Not that we will be able to tell some causal story, or even be able to identify the origins of some of our deepest attitudes; this is why we hypothesize a vignette from infancy, precisely because in most cases we will be unclear why we are deeply moved or motivated in certain respects.

a consciousness-raising group. Imagine her several years later, writing books on "The Starving Woman." She may even hold the view that the cultural imperative to be thin is a 'male plot' to subvert the energy of women: as long as women are preoccupied with avoiding food in order to achieve an emaciated norm they will have no energy left over to be writing books, getting advanced degrees, or promoting the cause of women in general.[18] But this newly constituted woman also carries a shameful secret: she still longs to be thin, and even though she knows that this view of women is destructive and manipulative, she is helplessly swayed by it.

If this person is not a hypocrite, or not simply self-deceived, we might conclude that she cannot get this atavistic portion of her personality to feel the way her reasoning makes her feel. When she thinks of millions of women enslaved by this self-image, she is outraged; when she thinks about her own deeper feelings, she is furious with herself. Nonetheless, the desire to be thin remains; her rage does not affect "the imprinted writing of many millennia." Which is not to say that it *cannot*. If this person lived for 80,000 years she would certainly have time to shift her deepest feelings. During that time the cultural norms would go through so many changes that she would be in a position to see, and more important, to feel, that such norms are transitory.[19] Of course, real women can only experience such norms as absolute, which, within the bounds of an average individual's life, they in fact usually are. In this sense a person's deepest feelings are a 'piece of fate'. "No one is accountable for existing at all, or for being constituted as he is, or for living in the circumstances and surroundings in which he lives . . . One is necessary, one is a piece of fate, one belongs to the whole."[20] *HOLISM*

Nietzsche's claims about a person's 'spiritual fate' may be interpreted as his apology (or at least his excuse) for the reprehensible remarks about women that follow it. Evidently, he thought that his deepest feelings about women were 'unteachable', and he completes *Beyond Good and Evil* 231 with the following comment: "I may perhaps be more readily permitted to utter a few truths about 'women as such'; assuming it is now understood from the outset to how great an extent these are only — *my* truths."[21] If his remarks about women are read without this preamble, they will certainly sound like truths, immutable truths at that; but, of course, Nietzsche denies that such truths exist. Our views may seem 'solid' (eter-

---

18. This is a view held by some feminists.
19. Nietzsche has much to say about these feelings in *Daybreak* 34, 35, and 103.
20. Nietzsche, "The Four Great Errors," in *Twilight of the Idols* 8.
21. Nietzsche, *Beyond Good and Evil* 231.

nal, essential) but they are no more solid than igneous rock — sturdy to be sure, but susceptible to erosion, earthquake, and human machinery.

It is clear — and, again, these introductory remarks are not offered as innovations — that Nietzche objects to the *metaphysical* claim that the terms 'subject', 'ego', 'soul', and 'human nature' make, and it is the metaphysical claim that he is attempting to subvert when he says that the aforementioned are 'fictions'. Clearly, people display enduring character traits, the sum total of which we may designate as 'character'. This character, however, has no metaphysical guarantee or grounding. 'Metaphysically' (if Nietzsche will even permit this nominal designation), a person is the potential for infinite variation, which is to say that no essence sets boundary conditions on the kind of self-interpretations we can undertake.[22] Not that we are therefore wildly self-interpreting, or that it is easy to undermine old convictions and take up new ones. As we saw in the case of our starving woman, it might be impossible. Here the Heidegger analog is useful. 'Human being' has the 'essence' of having no particular nature. Human beings are self-interpreting beings, and the possibilities for self-interpretation are limited (contingently) by local events rather than by an (absolute) inner nature.[23] Phenomenally, however, a person will display consistent and dependable character traits (his 'nature') that are altered only if something 'earthshaking' happens that can break up the granite of habituation and custom.

Writers of literary criticism often adduce Nietzsche's anti-essentialist remarks in order to advance some version of 'human being as cultural/social text', a text that can be revised, reconsidered, effaced, and reordered, especially in matters of gender. Although consideration of Nietzschean 'self-interpreting' must wait for Chapter 3, I want to say something here about a mistake that is often made when Nietzsche's denial of any essential human nature is so deployed. It is a mistake — and, in view of

---

22. Surely this is what Nietzsche means in the *Human, All Too Human* passage (41) when he says that in the "strict sense" one's character is not unchangeable. "Strict" evidently indicates something *akin* to a metaphysical account; in other words, this claim is as 'fundamental' as Nietzsche's explanations ever are.

23. Even though Heidegger's account is 'formal' (does not provide specific content for the notion 'human being') Nietzsche will resist giving an account such as this on the grounds that explanations *as such* are too reductive. In the previously quoted passage from *Twilight of the Idols* (8), Nietzsche goes on to remark that "no one gives a human being his qualities: not God, not society, not his parents or ancestors, not he himself . . . nothing exists apart from the whole." Hence Nietzsche's preference for 'interpretations', 'perspectives', and 'genealogies', all of which give accounts that are admittedly partial and incomplete. Heidegger's analytic method (and its debt to Kant's method) would be too comprehensive for Nietzsche's tastes.

Nietzsche's 'granitic' metaphor, a serious one — to treat the cultural accretions that contingently make up each person as 'soft', as opposed to the 'hard' data of biology, of genetic destiny. The reasoning perhaps goes as follows: cultural material is simply learned, while our genes are ineluctably given, and if gender turns out to be a cultural creation, rather than a biological one, then gender is revealed as something pliant, something that responds to our interpretive will. Of course, the initial assumption is misguided. Cultural material is often amazingly intractable, while the material biology provides can sometimes be altered in a surgical instant. Furthermore, that physical alteration, whether via the plastic surgeon's scalpel or through anorectic self-starvation, may not have any effect on a person's 'cultural inheritance'. As in the case of our starving woman, she may be objectively underweight while still seeing herself as fat.

Regardless of the reasoning behind it, many who adopt the language of 'person as text' seem to assume that rethinking the content of the text will inevitably alter that text. For example — and by no means the most egregious one — Lois McNay, in her critique of the use of Foucault's views in feminist ethics, says: "A political genealogy exposes the contingent and socially determined nature of sexuality, and, *thereby, frees the body* from the regulatory fiction of heterosexuality and opens up new realms in which bodily pleasures can be explored."[24] The properly Nietzschean response is: not necessarily. Exposing a 'regulatory fiction' may well liberate a person from its interpretive bounds; on the other hand, it may have no effect at all. To see that what moves and motivates you is part of a larger interpretive structure that creates certain objects of desire is not necessarily to be free of those desires. The question of what is and is not intractable in each person,[25] and why, is an utterly contingent matter, never answerable in theory, never answerable in advance of the specific reflective query at hand. Each person is, as Nietzsche lyrically puts it in "Schopenhauer as Educator," a "unique miracle . . . uniquely himself to every last movement of his muscles."[26]

Perhaps a better way to explain Nietzsche's 'denial of human nature' is the following: 'metaphysical' remarks, that is, remarks that claim to tell us something immutable and eternal about human beings, without reference to history, culture, physiology, or psychology, do not tell us anything. Nietzsche is certainly interested in the data that psychology and physiol-

---

24. Lois McNay, *Foucault and Feminism* (Boston: Northeastern University Press, 1993), p. 30; emphasis mine.

25. Cf. Judith Butler, *Gender Trouble* (New York: Routledge, 1990), p. 9.

26. Nietzsche, "Schopenhauer as Educator," in *Untimely Meditations*, section 1.

ogy will produce, but he will also object to the reification of such data as immutable scientific fact. It is not that scientific information is not true (indeed, Nietzsche held that his psychological observations were undoubtedly true), but it is not true in the scientist's (or, for that matter, the metaphysician's) decontextualized, permanent sense.

Thus far, we have made several useful distinctions in Nietzsche's model of the self. From the perspective of the individual, certain views, values, and attitudes are constitutive. Of course, this description is far too cognitive, since most of these 'attitudes' form the background for the attitudinal deliberations we usually associate with a person's character. These constitutive values are the 'unteachable granite' on which the more 'educable' loam rests. Alterations in a person normally take place at this level, although it is logically possible, though not likely, to alter the entire structure.

Charles Taylor, in his essay "What Is Human Agency?" outlines a structure remarkably similar to Nietzsche's. Taylor distinguishes between de facto, first-order desires, and the second-order desires, or evaluations, that we articulate vis-à-vis those de facto desires. These articulations are not simply descriptions of a 'fully independent object'. On the contrary, they are the voice of a person's struggle to express his deepest, and thus most elusive, feelings. Our starving woman's dilemma demonstrates how many important evaluations are confused and hidden. In struggling to understand why she finds some bodies more attractive than others, she is giving voice to these hidden feelings, and in so doing she is changing those feelings. Rather than being possessed of an inchoate uneasiness, she now has a number of psychological descriptions. Perhaps these descriptions activate other deeply held values that cause her to feel revulsion toward those newly articulated attitudes, and so on. Nietzsche would certainly concur that these foundational attitudes cannot be treated as existing discrete from the rest of the personality. As some parts of the character are altered, new 'horizons of value' emerge. "Altered opinions . . . do illuminate individual aspects of the constellation of his personality with which a different constellation of opinions had hitherto remained dark and unrecognizable."[27]

The attempt to express these deep feelings can, according to Taylor, move in two directions: a person may have a new sense of the experience at hand; conversely, that person may become more painfully aware of the limits of his fated 'granite'. Taylor's own example, that of a man fighting

---

27. Nietzsche, *Assorted Opinions and Maxims* 58.

obesity, demonstrates these two alternatives. If the man redescribes 'indulgence versus control' in terms of more or less satisfaction, rather than a spiritual battle against depraved gluttony, his recalcitrant cravings may lose their moral shrillness and will thus be easier to manage. However, this person, in so reformulating his struggle, may discover that in fact he is deeply committed to a moral view of his eating habits. He may realize that the moral dimension of his gustatory behavior is more essential to his view of himself than the first-order desire simply to lose weight.[28]

This 'deeply embedded shape' is, I claim, very much like Nietzsche's 'granite stratum of spiritual fate'. Imagine that Taylor's obese person *would like* to turn his efforts at dieting into a mere matter of satisfaction: eating less food, although an immediately less satisfying state, would ultimately result in a slimmer body, a more satisfying state of affairs, and his diet would thus be no more than a simple calculation of what will truly satisfy.[29] Even though this person wants to defuse the moral implications of his diet, however, *he may discover that he cannot.*

This notion of discovery is crucial. The implication is that each person is a series of cultural, familial, and social strata that can be explored, an undertaking that can be profoundly unsettling. Indeed, the possibility of discovery, discovery that in turn reveals more characteristics to be uncovered, is what distinguishes Nietzsche's view of a person.[30]

We might note how this view of Nietzsche differs from the received interpretation, which usually characterizes Nietzsche's great individual as endlessly self-creating rather than self-discovering. At the start of this chapter we found a first piece of evidence for the idea that the self, according to Nietzsche, is also receptive. A person's deeply embedded constitution is, to borrow from Taylor's account, the part of a person's character that 'receives' various attempts to redefine its (inchoate, unarticulated) sensibilities, but in so 'receiving' an articulation, a person's

---

28. Taylor remarks, "That description and experience are bound together in this constitutive relation admits of causal influences in both directions: it can sometimes allow us to alter experience by coming to fresh insight; but more fundamentally it circumscribes insight through the deeply embedded shape of experience for us" (*Human Agency and Language: Philosophical Papers 1* [Cambridge: Cambridge University Press, 1985], p. 37.)

29. That is, the second sort of satisfaction will persist over time in a way that the 'instant gratification' of eating will not.

30. It is interesting that Taylor does not see Nietzsche in this light. He writes, "The Nietzschean term 'value', suggested by our 'evaluation', carries this idea that our 'values' are our creations, that they ultimately repose on our espousing them." The extent to which a person's values can be manipulated, 'created' — that is, the limits of spiritual granite — is the subject of Chapter 3.

sense of his constitution is itself altered. Furthermore, the 'active' portion of a person's character is only the 'activity' that it is in terms of these embedded feelings. Chapter 3 characterizes this activity (namely, 'self-overcoming') and its relation to the 'receptive' portion of a person's character.

Nietzsche's view of a person's character has begun to emerge, but we now need to ask what kind of an account Nietzsche is giving. Once again we can usefully return to Heidegger's more pedagogical account of human being. Nietzsche certainly does not give us anything as programmatic as the existential analytic discussed in *Being and Time*, but he does seem to think that certain kinds of human behavior, such as 'reflecting' and 'self-overcoming', structure our cultural history as well as our daily lives. I call these remarks 'structural' because they do not inform us of recognizable, stable characteristics. More important, they do not evaluate particular actions. Consider, first, the kind of self-interest that Nietzsche calls 'vanity'. Earlier in this chapter I questioned the status of Nietzsche's aphorisms about vanity. How can vanity be part of the human constitution, when Nietzsche is claiming that no such constitution exists? Certainly, 'vanity' sounds as if it will be the quality 'V' that vain actions will always include, the consistently recognizable trait that vain people always exhibit. For Nietzsche, the Christian ascetic who starves and lacerates himself is vain. "This shattering of oneself, this scorn for one's own nature . . . which religions have made so much out of, is actually a high degree of vanity."[31] However, our ordinary notion of causality is also the product of vanity. "Is the goal, the 'purpose' not often enough a beautifying pretext, a self-deception of vanity after the event that does not want to acknowledge the ship is following the current into which it has entered accidentally?"[32] Self-abnegation, charity, passion, and virtue are also the work of vanity. If what we want is a generalizable description, the common feature that Nietzsche is identifying (whatever it may be) begins to look disappointingly vague.

Furthermore, 'vanity' can be either useful or useless, wise or stupid, base or noble. We are told that "originally [vanity] is the most useful of all things, the mightiest means of preservation,"[33] but we are also told that "there is nothing so reprehensible and unimportant in nature that it would not immediately swell up like a balloon at the slightest puff of the power of

---

31. Nietzsche, *Human, All Too Human* 137.
32. Nietzsche, *The Gay Science* 360.
33. Nietzsche, *The Wanderer and His Shadow* 181.

knowing."[34] A vain act does not, according to Nietzsche, have an intrinsic value because it is vain; that it is 'vain' merely tells us that self-interest is at work in some fashion. Whether or not that self-interest is noble, base, stupid, or useful will depend entirely on one's perspective. The account we give of a person's character is *itself* a perspective, and the grounds for claiming that the person in question is, among other things, vain will be part of the structure of that perspective.

Reflection, like vanity, is also an essential characteristic of human beings, and Nietzsche takes great pains to tell us how our view of ourselves can either save us or threaten to destroy us. According to Nietzsche, our reflective capacity is both the greatest boon and the greatest folly; sometimes it is merely the quality that makes us mediocre. 'Self-overcoming', which we may also hear as a capacity to re-evaluate our deepest values, is a structural potential that few of us have; 'self-overcoming' is a skill which the free spirits have mastered.

II

What does the 'granite stratum' indicate about the best sort of life to lead? How do we realize, fulfill, our contingently accreted natures? Are we meant to stand in opposition to the cultural materials that compose us, or must we simply give in to our 'deep stupidities', as Nietzsche seems to do in confessing his offensive views about women? What sort of ethical guidance does this account of human nature provide?

Of course, it is difficult, even by his own idiosyncratic lights, to cast Nietzsche in the role of ethical guide. He is generally — and quite rightly — regarded as the virtuoso iconoclast, cheerfully smashing our most deeply held views about morality, and this destruction is also taken to be his 'method' of moral critique. Nonetheless, it is crucial to see that Nietzsche is also quite the irritable ethicist, urging us to overcome our habitual lapses into self-deceived and despicable behavior.[35] If we focus on Nietzsche's

---

34. Nietzsche, "On Truth and Lies in a Non-Moral Sense," in *Philosophy and Truth: Selections from Nietzsche's Notebooks of the Early 1870's*, trans. Daniel Breazeale (Atlantic Highlands, N.J.: Humanities Press International, 1979), p. 79.

35. Philippa Foot notes that even though Nietzsche is rightly thought of as an 'immoralist', he nonetheless partakes of the moralist's fervor. "To this extent, then, Nietzsche is at one with the moralist: he is preaching self-discipline and control of the passions" ("Nietz-* sche: The Revaluation of Values," in *Nietzsche: A Collection of Critical Essays*, ed. Robert Solomon [Notre Dame: University of Notre Dame Press, 1980], p. 165).

consistent interest in circumspection (Besonnenheit), which he pro-
nounces "the virtue of virtues, their queen and great-grandmother,"[36]
his insistence on self-scrutiny and what we may banally call 'self-
improvement' (we should for the moment avoid morally loaded terms
such as 'virtue'), we can see a deeply traditional aspect of Nietzsche's
moral critique, namely, his commitment to the formation of character.
Nietzsche believes in character. He believes that a person's character can
be encouraged, refined, made beautiful. If a person's character is neglected, it will wither and become slothful, or worse yet, become moral.
"Out of passions grow opinions; mental laziness lets these rigidify into
convictions."[37] Moral systems and metaphysical principles are treated
with contempt; on the other hand, individuals who are disposed to act in
certain consistent ways (namely, individuals with a highly developed
character) are the objects of intense admiration. We find ourselves in
Nietzschean paradox. If we scorn all moral principles and regularities, if
we disallow all moral generalizations, how can we possibly nurture and
habituate a person's character? What sort of relation do the (idiosyncratic)
features of a person's character bear to their corresponding moral principles? If a person refuses to cheat on his income tax simply because it is
not in his character to do so, what relation does that act have to the moral
principle "It is wrong to cheat"?

Obviously, we are not yet in a position to answer these questions, but we
have made a start in understanding Nietzsche's moral critique. The end of
ethical action is not simply the performance of an ethical act, but the
shaping of an ethical *life*; each act plays a role in sculpting an entire ethical
terrain. To extend the metaphor, character allows us to describe, to calculate, to map. We can depend on various landmarks to be present in a
person, such as courage, temperance, and justice,[38] and the presence of
certain characteristics, such as courage and wisdom, is *enabling*. By developing these qualities a person is able to live more fully; the scope of her
choices is broader; she is able to live a better life. Refining one's character
and living 'the good life' are thus intimately connected. It is in a person's
interests to work on her character because a noble, beautiful character

---

36. Nietzsche, *The Wanderer and His Shadow* 294.

37. Nietzsche, *Human, All Too Human* 637. In 228 Nietzsche calls these individuals
'strong characters'.

38. Which is not to say that these are 'navigational' landmarks that guide a person. On the
contrary, when a person acts in a characteristic fashion, he does not 'steer' by certain
features, but simply acts in a 'usual' fashion: for example, the courageous person will simply
be courageous. It is this sort of typical display that creates a recognizable feature, just as a
familiar landscape will have characteristics that endure over time.

is the medium from which a good life emerges. Nietzsche realizes that this 'ethics of self-interest' is controversial, but he claims that it has ancient antecedents.

> Let us not deceive ourselves as to the motivation of that morality which demands difficulty of obedience to custom as the mark of morality! Self-overcoming is demanded, not on account of the useful consequences it may have for the individual, but so that the hegemony of custom, tradition shall be made evident. . . . Those moralists, on the other hand, who, following in the footsteps of Socrates, offer the *individual* a morality of self-control and temperance as a means to his own *advantage*, as his personal key to happiness, *are the exceptions.*[39]

The obvious ancestor is Aristotle. He too claimed that the creation of an excellent character was also the creation of the possibility of a good and happy life.[40] A good person's character is primarily composed of various behavioral dispositions, namely, virtues, that regulate passions and supervise judgment. The focus of Aristotle's investigation is the good life. Luck, habituation, and regulative character traits *serve us* (or fail to serve us) in obtaining happiness. Nietzsche agrees with this self-interested view of ethics, but he will disagree with Aristotle's account of the foundation of character, as well as with his understanding of what constitutes a happy life. Aristotle uses the concept of *ergon* (function) to establish a particular conception of the human good and the qualities that will facilitate this good. We move from the establishment of a characteristic function to the excellent performance of that function. The human good, Aristotle fa-

---

39. Nietzsche, *Daybreak* 9.

40. The comparison with Aristotle has little to do with the content of the views in question. The interesting similarity is the approach used. Nietzsche emulates the Aristotelian program of examining human behavior, and thinking about characteristic activity, *in order* to make ethical pronouncements that in turn have a close connection to the initial examination of human behavior. The 'typically' human and the 'good' for humans are thus closely aligned. Certainly, Nietzsche and Aristotle have often been compared, but usually on different grounds. Kaufmann sees Aristotle's conception of 'greatness of soul' as a tremendous influence in Nietzsche's work (*Nietzsche: Philosopher, Psychologist, Antichrist* [Princeton: Princeton University Press, 1974, p. 382]). Bernd Magnus, in his essay "Aristotle and Nietzsche: Megalopsychia and Übermensch," specifically takes Kaufmann to task on this matter. Magnus claims that the comparison with Aristotle's notion of megalopsychia is 'superficial', and that Nietzsche is more closely connected to Plato (*The Greeks and the Good Life*, ed. David J. Depew [Fullerton: California State University, 1979], p. 262). Chapter 1 has focused on the (formal) similarity of Nietzsche's program to Aristotle's; Chapter 4 will discuss a central feature of Nietzsche's debt to Plato.

mously concludes, is "an activity of soul in accordance with virtue, or if there are more kinds of virtue than one, in accordance with the best and most complete."[41]

Nietzsche's ethical remarks are also inextricably connected to what he takes our characteristic features to be. We are creatures of self-interest and absorption, and our 'vanity' is facilitated by our capacity to reason and to reflect critically on our behavior. But Nietzsche does not give us a sense of how these features work, or how best to nurture them, because he does not think that human nature has a coherent, legible structure. We cannot read a list of potential strengths and responsibilities from human nature, because our 'nature' is not fixed. Nietzsche has no objection to seeing human beings as having distinctive ends (that is, ends that are peculiarly human), but, as we have seen, he objects to the idea that these distinctive ends are determined by a fixed essence. Certainly, Nietzsche is at times a veritable cheerleader for the realization of what he takes to be our deepest and dearest human 'ends'.

> And so onwards along the path of wisdom, with a hearty tread, a hearty confidence! However you may be, be your own source of experience! Throw off your discontent about your nature . . . for you have in it a ladder with a hundred rungs, on which you can climb to knowledge . . . no honey is sweeter than that of knowledge.[42]

This knowledge is of course a species of self-knowledge, which might be better thought of as the way in which a person comes to understand herself. Nietzsche believes that all distinctively human capacities can be used to serve this goal of self-understanding, which Nietzsche also calls 'self-overcoming'. We are urged to overcome ourselves, to overcome our self-deceit and laziness, our tendency to believe and obey rather than to scrutinize and challenge. "My writings speak only of my overcomings: 'I' am in them, together with everything that was inimical to me. . . . One will divine that I already have a great deal—beneath me."[43] Certainly human beings have distinctive ends, but it is not clear how we will determine which ends are better than others (or even how to individuate and adequately characterize those ends), or how we will recognize 'self-knowledge' and then distinguish it from other kinds of human behavior.

---

41. Aristotle, *Nicomachean Ethics, The Basic Works of Aristotle*, trans. W. D. Ross (New York: Random House, 1941), I 1098a10–17.

42. Nietzsche, *Human, All Too Human* 292.

43. Nietzsche, *Assorted Opinions And Maxims*, preface.

At first glance, this program of 'climbing up' the obstacles of inclination and habit looks very much like the way in which the virtues work. Whatever deficiencies we have are corrected by the appropriate virtue: if a person is inclined to be miserly, he needs the corrective of generosity, and a person inclined to be timid needs a dose of courage. In the Aristotelian scheme of things, each person's requirements will be different, but the result (if successful) should resemble the paradigmatic virtuous person: all virtuous people will be just, kind, courageous, wise, and so on, in much the same ways, despite different temperaments and talents. Nietzsche will urge us to ascend his ladder of self-overcoming, but he denies that a univocal self waits at the top. His 'excellent characters' may seem not to resemble each other at all, for each will have his own, distinct sense of what qualities are required for his particular sort of excellence. "But the 'higher nature' of the great man lies in being different, in incommunicability . . . not in an effect of any kind—even if he made the whole globe tremble."[44] A review of the individuals that Nietzsche admires does not render a 'checklist' of qualities. In fact, the only obvious common feature among these men and (rarely) women is their stubborn commitment to being uniquely themselves, an enterprise that may not appear to be unique or remarkable at all.[45]

Nietzsche's denial of a univocal or paradigmatic 'person of excellence' is consistent with his skepticism about human nature in general. Aristotle begins with an account of human nature, and on that basis he provides a description of the way in which our intellectual and moral capacities can develop and flourish. A person who has developed these capacities has therefore realized his human potential, and the account comes full circle. Nietzsche, on the other hand, doubts that there are essential human features that can be realized in this way, and he heaps scorn on all such essentialist doctrines. Nietzsche exhorts us to realize ourselves—here Nietzsche sounds most Aristotelian—but it seems that the nature we are to 'realize' is no nature at all.[46] Because human nature is indeterminate, we will not be able to render an Aristotelian conclusion about what the good for human beings will be, nor will we be able to describe a 'best activity'. For Aristotle, an investigation of human nature reveals our distinctive feature, rationality, and the ultimate developmental principle is

---

44. Nietzsche, *The Will to Power* 876.

45. Alexander Nehamas gives an eloquent account of Nietzsche's 'great characters' in his *Nietzsche: Life as Literature* (Cambridge: Harvard University Press, 1985). I will have more to say about these characters in Chapter 4.

46. Cf. the third of the *Untimely Meditations*, "Schopenhauer as Educator."

that we act in accordance with that rational capacity. If a person is properly nurtured and habituated, and if things don't go too badly for him, he will become a person who lives wisely and well, and in specific and recognizable ways. Not everybody will be able to achieve this level of ethical achievement, and for obvious reasons: not everyone will have adequate parenting, or the proper education, or even the good fortune (such as being a male) necessary to become a *phronimos.*

Likewise, Nietzsche scrutinizes human behavior in order to determine what sort of life is worth living, but he denies that any fixed essence underlies the wide range of human activities. Nonetheless, certain formal features of being human can be identified, and Nietzsche claims that only the full exploitation of these features will result in an admirable life. Nietzsche also believes that this full life will not, and moreover, cannot, be attained by all human beings. Each human being will have his own idiosyncratic history, with its own issues and complications; this is the 'nature' that each person is called to 'overcome'. But not everyone will rise to this level of achievement, and in each case the reasons for failure or success will be different. Social scientists and historians will not be able to identify the Übermensch as easily as they can recognize the *phronimos.* More important, the very notions of recognition, identification, 'marks and features', are perhaps inimical to the undertaking Nietzsche describes.

In other words, Aristotle's investigation of human beings reveals a rational, educable function, while Nietzsche's reveals a nonrational, largely uneducable fate. Each, on the basis of his findings, prescribes a program. Aristotle emphasizes training, upbringing, the development of appropriate sensibilities, while Nietzsche urges each person to embrace his fated constitution in the necessary fashion. Of course, the 'necessary fashion' cannot be determined in advance of the individual who must come to terms with himself. Finally, that self-examination will not reveal a set of principles that 'rationalize' a person's constitution. The contingency of the composition of the self is the only 'essential principle' to be found.

III

So, what are these 'accretions'? What kinds of material are 'cultural strata' made of? A first and obvious candidate is value; indeed this notion is a confusing one (although in the course of our investigation we will inevitably encounter another, even more obscure possibility, the will to power). We might begin by provisionally defining value as "things held to be desirable and good by the human community." However, this banal description of value only serves to highlight the problem of why Nietzsche focuses his energies on both the overturning and the 'revaluing' of value. Why would Nietzsche, who is skeptical of all value, particularly those unconditionally held, want to investigate the value of values?[47] Of course, to ask this question is simply to raise once again the question of value, which for Nietzsche is inseparable from the question of evaluation. "Evaluation is creation: hear it, you creative men! Valuating is itself the value and jewel of all valued things."[48] In observing the 'value of evaluation', the obscurity of the essential notion; namely, value itself, becomes even more pressing.

Certainly, Heidegger felt that the considerable attention given to the concept of value by philosophers revealed only a lack of understanding in the matter. He poses the following questions for Nietzsche: "What does Nietzsche understand by value? . . . Why is Nietzsche's metaphysics the metaphysics of values?"[49] We should be struck by the boldness of Heidegger's implicit claim: how can Nietzsche, the consummate antimetaphysician, have a 'metaphysics of value'? Why does Heidegger believe that this 'metaphysical' importance of value in Nietzsche's thinking leads to a nihilism in which no one 'would die for mere value'? How is it that the things we find deeply meaningful are reduced by attaining the status of a 'value'?

According to Heidegger, values are the result of calculations made by the will to power: a value is an articulation of whatever a configuration of forces needs to maintain itself *as* that particular configuration of forces. Even art can be seen as just such a marshalling of forces, the 'condition' posited by the will to power. This 'conditioning' is 'metaphysical' because these values are taken to be the fundamental units of reality, of Being:

47. For example, Nietzsche, *The Genealogy of Morals*, trans. Walter Kaufmann and R. J. Hollingdale (New York: Vintage Books, 1967), preface, section 6, and *Twilight of the Idols*, preface, are two important statements of 'revaluation'.

48. Nietzsche, "On the Thousand and One Goals," in *Thus Spake Zarathustra*. I will have more to say about this passage at the end of the chapter.

49. Heidegger, "The Word of Nietzsche: God is Dead," in *The Question Concerning Technology and Other Essays*, trans. William Lovitt (New York: Harper and Row, 1977), who writes, "We speak of the values of life, of cultural values, of eternal values, of the hierarchy of values, of spiritual values. . . . We build systems of values and pursue in ethics classifications of values. . . . We hold science to be value-free and relegate the making of value judgments to the sphere of world views. . . . The frequency of talk about values is matched by a corresponding vagueness of the concept" (pp. 70–71).

> If metaphysics must in its utterance exhibit that which is, in respect to Being, and if therewith after its manner it names the ground of that which is, then the grounding principle of the metaphysics of the will to power must state this ground. . . . The grounding principle of the metaphysics of the will to power is a value-principle.[50]

'Reality' is thus an ordering of beliefs, desires, and concomitant practices that preserve and promote particular manifestations of the will to power. What, then, is the will to power? Heidegger asserts that the 'will to power' is better understood as the 'will to will'; that is, rather than imagining 'a being that wills power', we should imagine a *will*, creating a structure of value. "What the will wills it has already. For the will wills its will."[51] To describe 'will to power' as a 'will' looking for 'power' is much like describing an eye as 'looking' for vision. Eyes *see*, and the will to power *wills*. Furthermore, that will has no goal outside of itself in terms of which it understands itself. Will is simply willing; its ends are provisional and incidental. The 'will to will' articulates and promotes the values that enhance its own ends; as such, these values are not the discrete, objective goods that the notion 'value' generally suggests (for example, 'the value of justice').[52]

We may draw two preliminary conclusions about Heidegger's reading of Nietzschean value. First, he sees values as constituents of a will to power metaphysic. Second, as these constituents they are essentially *compromised*. A value is never impartial or uninterested, despite its supporters who would characterize the value in question as 'unassailable', 'natural', 'dictated by reason', and so forth.[53] It is easy then to see why one might

---

50. Ibid., p. 86.

51. Ibid., p. 77. Cf. these remarks from Heidegger's Nietzsche lectures: "What does 'will' mean? What does 'will to power' mean? For Nietzsche these two questions are but one. For in his view will is nothing else than will to power, and power is nothing else than the essence of will" (*Nietzsche*, vol. 1: *The Will to Power as Art*, trans. David Farrell Krell [London: Routledge and Kegan Paul, 1981], 37).

52. Michel Haar offers these remarks about Heidegger's interpretation of will to power:

> Values in general are conditions posed by the 'calculating aim of the Will to Power', its conservation and its incessant reinforcement. They are not free and disinterested creations but conditions of existence, knowingly calculated. The Will to Power sets values according to a calculation that aims to insure the survival and intensification of its force.

"The Doubleness of the Unthought of the Overman: Ambiguities of Heideggerian Political Thought," trans. Lang Baker, unpublished manuscript.

53. Nietzsche would not disagree with the latter half of this characterization; indeed, the seedy history of every value is its 'genealogy'.

find either of these qualities objectionable; however, the fundamental Heideggerian objection is a more complicated matter. The will to will, as a force establishing and enforcing value, operates according to a particular logic, the logic of self-overcoming. The will posits values, and takes up certain values, in order to 'overcome' them: that is, to explore a value (and the way of life that value entails) to the point of its own exhaustion. The will is essentially self-overcoming; the values taken up by the will are taken up in order to be overcome.[54] This notion of a will that understands itself to be taking up values in order that they might be overcome is, Heidegger claims, utter nihilism.

> But what happens to value-positing itself when value-positing is thought in respect to that which is as such, and that means at the same time from out of a view toward Being? Thus, thinking in terms of values is radical killing.[55]

What has been killed is the possibility of some inarticulable, nonrepresentational, noncalculable source from which that which is valued emerges. Everything becomes available for the will's inexorable consumption. 'Value' becomes nothing more than a kind of conceptual detritus, a label indicating where deeper springs of human action once existed. As such, values are completely objectified and represented; they consist of consciously posited representations.

> The uprising of man into subjectivity transforms that which is into object. But that which is objective is that which is brought to a stand through representing. The doing away with that which is in itself, i.e., the killing of God, is accomplished in the making secure of the constant reserve by means of which man makes secure for himself material, bodily, psychic, and spiritual resources . . . Making secure, as the creating of secureness, is grounded in value-positing.[56]

This act of hyper-articulation has consequences for the human character. Heidegger sees the positing of value as a process that flattens our deepest cultural sensibilities and turns shared practices into placards. "Being has

---

54. I have more to say about this 'logic' of value overcoming itself in Chapters 3 and 4.

55. Heidegger, "The Word of Nietzsche," in *The Question Concerning Technology and Other Essays*, p. 108.

56. Ibid., p. 107.

been transformed into a value."[57] 'Values' are the well-formed products of reflection. As the coins of *Gerede*, of the daily commerce of articulation, they can no longer deeply move us; hence, Heidegger's declaration that "no one dies for mere values."[58]

In order to clarify the struggle between the forces of articulation and our inarticulable cultural sensibilities, we may borrow some terminology from another of Heidegger's later essays, namely, the strife between 'earth' and 'world'. Here is Heidegger's own metaphorical account:

> This Open happens in the midst of beings. It exhibits an essential feature which we have already mentioned. To the Open there belongs a world and the earth . . . the world is the clearing of the paths of the essential guiding directions with which all decision complies. Every decision, however, bases itself on something not mastered, something concealed, confusing; else it would never be a decision. The earth is not simply the Closed but rather that which rises up as self-closing. World and earth are always intrinsically and essentially in conflict, belligerent by nature.[59]

'World' is the force that would make explicit our deepest beliefs and practices; 'world' represents, articulates, scrutinizes, calculates, judges, deliberates, and, ultimately, alters those beliefs and practices. 'Earth' is the the cultural source of those articulations and representations; as such, it resists the willful efforts of 'world' to make its constitution into a network of beliefs and desires. 'World' would have all things be comprehensible, ordered, which is why 'it cannot endure anything closed'; 'earth' is that which is nonrationalizable in this way. In defending an ethical view, for example, an interlocutor will at some point resort to that infamous re-source, her 'intuitions'. This inchoate sense of what is essential in her argument is its 'earth', while the rules, stipulations, and philosophical architecture of her view are its 'worldliness'. Furthermore, in her act of giving a structure to those intuitions, she undeniably refines and alters them.[60]

Will to power, as the positing of value, is anathema to Heidegger's

---

57. Ibid., p. 102.

58. Heidegger, "The Age of the World Picture," in *The Question Concerning Technology and Other Essays*, p. 142.

59. Heidegger, "The Origin of the Work of Art," in *Poetry, Language, Thought*, trans. Albert Hofstadter (New York: Harper and Row, 1971), p. 55.

60. Cf. Charles Taylor's description of how a person expresses deep yet primarily inarticulate sensibilities:

'understanding of being' because it places human representations at the center of what is meaningful. The will to will renders everything in terms of 'world', and abolishes the 'earth'. Heidegger sees the Übermensch as the most sophisticated version of this nihilistic pursuit of value: indeed, as the ultimate free spirit. "Man whose essence is that essence which is willing, i.e., ready, from out of the will to power is overman."[61] The Übermensch transforms his cultural practices into a series of representations, which are thus available as commodities to be manipulated and used up.

> In this revolutionary objectifying of everything that is the earth, that which first of all must be put at the disposal of representing and setting forth, moves into the midst of human positing and analysing. The earth itself can show itself only as the object of assault, an assault that, in human willing, establishes itself as unconditional objectification.[62]

At last we have arrived at Heidegger's deepest objection to the 'will to power metaphysic'. The Übermensch is problematic not simply because he wants to objectify (and thus diminish) cultural concerns, but because he would consume these flattened concerns *for the sake of* erecting more value-representations, which are in turn exhausted *for the sake of a different* set of values. This process of establishing value/consuming value is, according to Heidegger, the essence of the 'will to will', and is the fullest flowering of its inherent nihilism.

Heidegger's account of Nietzsche is, to say the least, an unappealing one, but it raises an important question for our investigation. Is Nietzsche's model of the ideal human self that of the 'hyper-evaluator', positing values in order to undermine them? Or, to frame this question in the terms established in the Preface, is Nietzsche's ideal self 'active' rather than 'receptive'? Is the Übermensch a *maker* of value, or an *expression* of his culture's deepest concerns?

Our attempts to formulate what we hold important must, like descriptions, strive to be faithful to something. But what they strive to be faithful to is not an independent object with a fixed degree and manner of evidence, but rather a largely inarticulate sense of what is of decisive importance. An articulation of this 'object' tends to make it something different from what it was before.

Charles Taylor, *Human Agency and Language: Philosophical Papers 1* (Cambridge: Cambridge University Press, 1985), p. 38. I will say more about this aspect of Taylor's views in a moment.
  61. Heidegger, "The Word of Nietzsche," p. 96.
  62. Ibid., p. 100.

The task of this book is to suggest how it is that Nietzsche's ideal individual is active as well as receptive (hence, Nietzsche's use of active/receptive pairs of metaphors in describing this individual). This supreme individual is one who understands himself as composed of *both* the activity of 'world' and the receptivity of 'earth'. Again, Heidegger inadvertently provides us with an excellent model for understanding Nietzsche. Although the arguments for this view should be left to the appropriate chapters, I want to make a few general observations about value and the problems it generates, particularly some concerns about skepticism.

Nietzsche certainly admired the skeptical intellect, and its attendant powers of reflection (that is, the free spirit's ability to place concepts before himself in thought). These remarks from *Twilight of the Idols* 54 are characteristic:

> One should not let oneself be misled: great intellects are sceptics. Zarathustra is a sceptic. The vigor of a mind, its freedom through strength and superior strength, is proved by scepticism. Men of conviction simply do not come into consideration where the fundamentals of value and disvalue are concerned. Convictions are prisons. They do not see far enough, they do not see things beneath them: but to be permitted to speak about value and disvalue one must see five hundred convictions beneath one . . . behind one.

The sort of 'world'-like scrutiny detailed in Heidegger's account is certainly suggested by this passage; the more vigorous free spirits will take up, investigate, and exhaust as many values as possible. Besides *this* sort of robust activity, however, the passage also suggests another dimension of experience, one that is not captured by either the skepticism of the free spirit or the convictions of the higher men. Indeed, the free spirit who is permitted to 'speak about value' must be able to see the convictions that are 'beneath' and 'behind' him. He must be able to see the values that have made him the individual he is. This sort of 'constitutive' value would be very different from the 'convictions' that imprison, because *these* values have yet to be represented, articulated. They are, in Heidegger's terms, more like 'earth' and less like 'world': in and as constitutive value they are not yet the sort of 'value' that Heidegger despises.[63]

Daybreak 534 makes a related observation:

---

63. Again, Taylor's notion of the 'inchoate sense' out of which our strong articulations of value emerge is certainly an example of values that 'constitute' a person; which is to say, 'values' that are not yet expressed *as* values.

Small doses. — If a change is to be as profound as it can be, the means to it must be given in the smallest doses but unremittingly over long periods of time! Can what is great be created in a single stroke? So let us take care not to exchange the state of morality to which we are accustomed for a new evaluation of things head over heels and amid acts of violence — no, let us continue to live in it for a long, long time yet — until, probably a long while hence, we become aware that the new evaluation has acquired predominance within us and that the little doses of it . . . have laid down a new nature in us.

This passage champions a process that is very different from the willful, manipulative articulations of (Heidegger's version of) the Übermensch. Rather than the free spirit 'taking command' of a particular value, Nietzsche recommends that he allow this value to 'take command' of himself. Clearly, this new evaluation has its own power that may work on, and in, the free spirit, regardless of how the free spirit conceives of that evaluation. Nietzsche evidently believes that values have a kind of power or force of their own; with this preliminary conclusion in mind we may consider what Nietzsche says in *The Gay Science* 301: "Only we have created the world that concerns man!"

Despite our acknowledgment that the origin of all value is found in the concerns and struggles of human activity, we may *not* therefore conclude that value can be legislated in and out of existence by reflecting on that activity. This conclusion is disallowed for two reasons.

First, Nietzsche is skeptical about the very powers of reason that would undertake this deconstruction and reconstruction of value. Certainly, the human intellect is powerful; but neither is it all-powerful nor does the intellect necessarily understand the scope and limits of its powers:

> This intellect has no additional mission which would lead it beyond human life. Rather, it is human, and only its possessor and begetter takes it so solemnly — as though the world's axis turned within it. But if we could communicate with the gnat, we would learn that he likewise flies through the air with the same solemnity, that he feels the flying center of the universe within himself . . . this pride contains within itself a most flattering estimation of the value of knowing. Deception is the most general effect of such pride.[64]

---

64. Nietzsche, "On Truth and Lies in a Nonmoral Sense," in Breazeale, *Philosophy and Truth: Nietzsche's Early Notebooks*, p. 79.

Nietzsche's admiration for the human intellect is thus qualified in a telling fashion. He may admire the human intellect, but not simply because the intellect displays a variety of powers — that sort of admiration is the self-deceiving pride that Nietzsche mocks. Rather, as we previously saw in the passage from *Ecce Homo*, the faculty of reason finds its ultimate expression in the exercise of its skeptical abilities, yet the skeptic is inevitably engaged in uncovering the feebleness and self-deception of the intellect and the sorts of compromises to which reason must resign itself. The greatness of the intellect thus lies in its ability to understand its own shortcomings and limits: which is to say, not primarily in feats of *either* intellectual construction or deconstruction. The projects of establishing value on the one hand (by the 'higher men' of *Thus Spake Zarathustra*) or destroying value on the other (by the free spirits) are both susceptible to self-deception and delusion. The well-asked question, however, the question that illuminates — indeed, the sort of question that both the building and tearing down of value require — is, according to Nietzsche, the finest moment of the human intellect.

Second, the reason why value cannot simply be destroyed and reinvented, so to speak, at will, lies in a point that has already been suggested: the free spirits who attack the evaluations of their culture are themselves cultural products. The free spirits must come to terms with themselves at the same time as they rebuke the age that produced them.

> Have you never been plagued by the fear that you might be completely incapable of knowing the truth? The fear that your mind may be too dull and even your subtle faculty of seeing still much too coarse? Have you noticed what kind of will rules behind your seeing? . . . Have you sometimes looked for something which affected you strongly, sometimes for what soothed you — because you happened to be tired! . . . As though you were able to traffic with things of thought any differently from the way you do with men! In this traffic too there is the same morality, the same honorableness, the same reservations, the same slackness, the same timidity — your whole loveable and hateful ego! . . . Do you not fear to re-encounter in the cave of every knowledge your own ghost — the ghost which is the veil behind which truth has hidden itself from you?[65]

The person who begins an investigation will ultimately 'investigate' himself. The questions he poses and the issues he raises are themselves an

---

65. Nietzsche, *Daybreak* 539.

indication of his interests, aspirations, and struggles. For our concerns, the point here is the status of the person vis-à-vis the values he holds. The Heideggerian claim is that the Übermensch will be able to select, take up, and exhaust a value as he likes. But the above passage by Nietzsche indicates that the very constitution of the individual prohibits this sort of value manipulation. Value cannot be 'shopped for' when needed and 'discarded' when used up because individuals are not distinct from the values they hold in the way that a purchaser is distinct from his purchases. Because individuals are not distinct from the values they hold, it is unclear what would be 'chosen' in so choosing a value, or 'discarded' in the rejection of a value. If a person is *composed* of values, then the account of how it is that they create and reject value will necessarily be more complicated. Indeed, the metaphor of 'spiritual granite' indicates a host of processes older and more profound than any 'surface tilling'.

In the course of this discussion I have basically identified two senses of 'value'. There are values as they are ordinarily conceived, the claims about justice, goodness, truth, and so on, that we articulate and endorse. Value in the second sense of the notion is not divided into 'values'; rather, it constitutes the very choices with which the first sort of value presents us. The practices and presuppositions of a culture form this kind of inchoate value, out of which particular evaluations emerge. Now, this useful distinction between what we may now call 'active' and 'receptive' senses of 'value' might seem to imply a reification of value. On the one hand, there are actual values that can be created and promulgated; on the other, a set of forces that shape and constitute whole cultures and ages.

Any such metaphysical understanding of the role that value plays in Nietzsche's texts is, however, undermined by the presence of another of his views, perspectivism. We will temporarily define perspectivism as Nietzsche's claim that our representations, accounts, and bodies of investigative methods cannot provide a whole or absolute understanding of reality. No decontextualized, immutable truths can be established because no representation is complete (even by the lights of its own investigative goals) or final. Values cannot emerge from, say, a set of foundational truths, since no such truths exist; instead, values are created by particular perspectives. "Insight: all evaluation is made from a definite perspective: that of the preservation of the individual, a community, a race, a state, a church, a faith, a culture."[66] We may, as an initial approximation, see values as that which a particular perspective has as its aim or object. "Willing means

---

66. Nietzsche, *The Will to Power* 259.

willing an end. 'An end' includes an evaluation."[67] Since perspectives are selective the values they generate will also be bound by their selective, perspectival considerations. Values will thus have a history that expresses particular interests and motives. "The deeper one looks the more our valuations disappear . . . we have created the world that possesses values!"[68]

But values and perspectives are a tangled and incestuous lot, for we might also see their roles as reversed. A perspective can also be understood as a complex of value. The deep evaluations created by socialization and cultural history, out of which the values we actively formulate actually arise, may indeed constitute what we may call a person's perspective. If, for example, two individuals discover that they have a particular value in common, then it must be the case that an unspoken host of values is already shared in order for that value to show up for both of them *as* that particular value. If these individuals share enough values, both apparent and deep, then we might say that they have the same perspective (of course, this in turn depends on our reasons for comparing the views of these particular individuals in the first place). The essential point here is that 'value' can be heard quite broadly, perhaps as 'way of life' on the one hand, or as 'perspectival constituent' on the other. In identifying the notion of value as bound up with that of perspective, however, we have effectively limited the sort of claims we may make about value. The nature, scope, and force of a value or set of values will, quite simply, be a matter of the perspective in question.

We might consider how Heidegger explains the relations between perspectivism and value in Nietzsche's writings. Heidegger claims that 'perspective' is just another cog in the machinery of will to power.

> Value is value inasmuch as it counts. It counts inasmuch as it is posited as that which matters. It is so posited through an aiming at and a looking toward that which has to be reckoned upon. . . . The essence of everything that is . . . lays hold of itself in this way and posits for itself an aim in view. That aim provides the perspective that is to be conformed to. The aim in view is value.

'Value' is thus the 'aim' of a perspective; in this sense the 'essence' of value is that it is a 'point-of-view'. Heidegger is quite clear that 'value' and 'point-of-view' are 'equiprimordial': one does not exist independent of the other,

67. Ibid., 260.
68. Ibid., 602.

nor does one come into being before the other. "Values, therefore, are not antecedently something in themselves so that they can on occasion be taken as points-of-view."[69] Although Heidegger is right to insist that Nietzsche sees 'perspective' and 'value' as interdependent, I suggest that he does not take the enterprise of perspectivism as radically as Nietzsche intended it. Although a critique of perspectivism itself must wait, I shall make a few suggestions here about Heidegger's (mis)understanding of 'value' and 'perspectivism'.

Heidegger's formulaic account seems to suggest that perspective just is the positing 'gaze' that 'aims' at a value: to understand a perspective, we need only take stock of the values held in a particular point-of-view. Nietzsche would certainly deny that a set of values 'constitutes' a perspective; in fact, he asserts that perspectives are seriously beyond our reckoning.

> How far the perspective character of existence extends, or indeed whether existence has any character than this; whether existence without interpretation, without sense, does not become 'nonsense'; whether, on the other hand, all existence is not essentially actively engaged in interpretation — that cannot be decided even by the most industrious and most scrupulously conscientious analysis and self-examination of the intellect; for in the course of this analysis the human intellect cannot avoid seeing itself in its own perspectives, and only in these.[70]

Heidegger claims that a perspective is the 'sight' that places a value as a goal, but this infamous passage indicates that a perspective is, for Nietzsche, somehow beyond all of the values that we could predicate of it, and that in our examination of the values articulated by a perspective. We keep revealing more about that which we value, but very little about the perspective as such. Heidegger's account seems to assume that 'perspectives' are as highly articulated as 'values', and he describes a series of perspectives rather as though they were a row of coin-operated binoculars pointed at a landmark: by 'looking toward' a particular aim, you adopt a perspective and its attendant value. "The aim provides the perspective that is to be conformed to."[71]

Again, we have yet to consider an analysis of perspectivism; however, for the moment I end with the suggestion that 'perspective' is not some-

---

69. Heidegger, "The Word of Nietzsche," p. 72.
70. Nietzsche, *The Gay Science* 74.
71. Heidegger, "The Word of Nietzsche," p. 72.

thing that can be located via a value, but something we are always already in, and always engaged in getting clear about. Perspectives are perhaps more like Heideggerian 'earth', with only a fraction of a perspective being truly 'wordly': that is, with only a bit of it so highly articulated that it can be picked out as a 'value'. Michel Haar makes this elegant summation:

> The Nietzschean philosophy is not fundamentally a philosophy of representation: it is, rather, a philosophy of interpretation. Interpretation, or the 'perspectivism' of values, understood as an indefinite and infinite process is opposed at once to any hold upon a substantial reality as it would be in itself. . . . Heidegger's repeated use of the term 'calculation' (Berechnung) with respect to values can only be taken metaphorically inasmuch as for Nietzsche this calculation is not right or wrong, true or false . . . the interpretive power cannot set up its interpretations like a tableaux, like something represented to it, for *it is itself its interpretations*.[72]

Haar's assertion directs us away from 'calculation', 'representation', 'positing', and re-introduces the rather more twilit uncertainties of interpretation, much of which is not a reflective activity. Heidegger's account implies that a person may calculate which values he will take up, and, by 'aiming' at them, adopt the necessary perspective. (As in our previous metaphor, a quay-side stroller may select what he wants to see and view it by taking the appropriate binocular aim: the perspective merely is seeing what is to be seen.)

If values are not (contra Heidegger) obvious candidates for essential metaphysical units in Nietzsche's thinking, then what about the will to power, the force on whose behalf, according to Heidegger, those values are deployed? Indeed, although value will be a recurrent issue in this work, the will to power will not.[73] The following remarks provide a few suggestions about its status.

We can distinguish between two types of explanations of the will to power. One, a standard offering, asserts that ascriptions of the will to power is merely the observation that human resources and events are controlled by individuals who have 'power', either in the straightfor-

---

72. Haar, "The Doubleness of the Unthought of the Overman," 26; emphasis mine.

73. Likewise, the collection of notes that bears that name. I find Heidegger's dependence on these unpublished fragments questionable; I am certainly more interested in Nietzsche's published 'thought' than in his 'unthought' (Heidegger's term for what he sees as the implicit claims of Nietzsche's texts, which Heidegger quite often 'discovers' in Nietzsche's notebooks). See my References.

wardly physical sense, or some more complex admixture of intellect, brawn, persuasion, money, social status, and so forth. A second sort of account views the will to power (in a somewhat Schopenhauerian spirit) as some sort of cosmic principle or guiding constitutive force. We may call the assertion of the will to power on the first sort of view the 'vulgar thesis', and, on the second, the 'trivial thesis'.

We start with the 'trivial thesis', since it is perhaps the less persuasive of two unfortunate candidates. This account — so called because it manages to turn the will to power into a trivial claim — is generated by several very obscure passages. Nietzsche sometimes seems to mysticize the will to power, indicating that 'everything' is will to power. "The world seen from within, the world described and defined according to its 'intelligible character' — it would be will to power and nothing more."[74] Similarly, in *The Will to Power* 689 Nietzsche asks the following question: "Should we not be permitted to assume this will as a motive cause in chemistry too? — and in the cosmic order?" Thus, the will to power would be the quality common to alteration, generation, corruption: every sort of action and reaction, from earthquake to revolution, would be an instance of the will to power.

This 'trivial thesis' is untenable (by Nietzsche's own lights, as we shall see) for an obvious reason: it empties the concept 'will to power' of any significance. If 'everything' is will to power, then how do attributions of it say anything distinctive about the world, or human nature? When Nietzsche observes, as he often does, that a particular action, person, or quality displays a high degree of will to power, what can such an attribution mean, since indeed 'everything' is will to power? Consider a physical analogy: we might say that all matter is 'a lattice of moving particles', but we could not distinguish between, for example, a table and a block of iron by picking out the iron as a 'higher degree' of moving particles, or having 'more matter' — both the table and the metal block are instances of matter, and neither is a greater or lesser display of matter as such. Of course, we might then want to distinguish one object as having more mass, or being more dense; however, these distinctions do not indicate that one object 'matters' more than the other. If will to power is truly as elemental as some readers of Nietzsche (as well as some of Nietzsche's own rather confusing remarks) claim, then it cannot do the kind of work that Nietzsche requires of it.

---

74. Nietzsche, *Beyond Good and Evil* 36. Notice that the statement is a conditional: *if* the world *could* be seen from within, it *would* be will to power and nothing else. Certainly, the little I have said about perspectivism already indicates that no such essential point of view is possible.

We might detrivialize the view somewhat by seeing the will to power as a basic force that comes in 'forms', just as matter can be thought of as having essentially three phases: gas, liquid, and solid. The will to power might thus have analogous forms, such as 'spiritual',[75] 'physical', and 'aesthetic'. However, this notion of some 'essence' that enters into many forms is one that Nietzsche explicitly denies. Indeed, this sort of constitutive force variously manifested sounds remarkably like Schopenhauer's 'will', and Nietzsche clearly did not see the will to power as this sort of metaphysical thesis.

> Is 'will to power' a kind of 'will' or identical with the concept 'will'? Is it the same thing as desiring? or commanding? Is it that 'will' of which Schopenhauer said it was the 'in-itself' of all things? . . . My proposition is: that the will of psychology is an unjustified generalization, that this will does not exist at all, that instead of grasping the idea of the development of one definite will into many forms, one has eliminated the character of the will by subtracting it from its content, its 'whither'? — this . . . is the case with Schopenhauer: what he calls 'will' is merely an empty word. It is even less a question of a 'will to live'; for life is merely a special case of the will to power; it is quite arbitrary to assert that everything strives to enter into this form of the will to power.[76]

We might hear this passage as follows: in describing one will as taking many forms, Schopenhauer inadvertently empties the notion of meaning by separating it from its content. He cannot (according to Nietzsche) think of will apart from its content; 'will' is not distinct from what is willed. This 'subtraction' is impossible because it posits an unjustified totality. "There is no 'totality'; . . . no evaluation of human existence, of human aims, can be made in regard to something that does not exist."[77] A more famous passage also expresses this idea:

> For just as popular mind separates the lightning from its flash and takes the latter for an action, for the operation of a subject called lightning, so popular morality also separates strength from expressions of strength, as if there were a neutral substratum behind the strong man,

---

75. Nietzsche, *Beyond Good and Evil*.
76. Nietzsche, *The Will to Power* 692.
77. Ibid., 711.

which was free to express its strength or not to do so. But there is no such substratum; there is no 'being' behind doing, effecting, becoming; the 'doer' is merely a fiction added to the deed.[78]

Likewise, there is no 'will to power' behind acts or instances of will to power. This dictum follows from Nietzsche's thoroughgoing antimetaphysicalism, of which I will say more in the next chapter. We must be wary of any claims about the will to power that generalize it as a contentless force 'behind' a multitude of forms.

The 'vulgar' account, on the other hand, provides too much content, at least of a particular sort. This kind of view claims that the will to power is domination, thus every act of will to power is an act of domination. The unsophisticated version of this view simply refers us to 'brute force'. When Nietzsche expresses his admiration for the will to power he is admiring an instance of strength prevailing over weakness, the strong noble versus the weak slave.[79] Obviously, this account says less about the will to power displayed by the artist, the ascetic, and even the priestly class. More sophisticated views extend the notion of 'domination' (via the notion of 'sublimation') in order to accomodate the many sorts of artistic and cultural endeavors in which Nietzsche sees the will to power at work. Thus, Walter Kaufmann remarks:

> The will to power is thus not only the devil who diverts man from achieving culture, or a psychological urge that helps to explain diverse and complex types of human behavior . . . instead of being associated primarily with neurotics who crave pity, with modern man's lust for money, with the burning of heretics and good books . . . the will to power may now be envisaged as the basic drive of all human efforts. Philosophic discourse, the ancient tragedies and comedies, the Platonic dialogues . . . are all understood in terms of the Greeks' will to outdo, excel and overpower one another. . . . Political and cultural

---

78. Nietzsche, *The Genealogy of Morals*, Essay I, 13. Tracy Strong makes the same point: "The will to power refers then not to an ontological principle, nor to something that has evolved. . . . *It is rather the movement itself*, and thus has neither being nor becoming. It can only be understood in terms of its 'whither' " (*Friedrich Nietzsche and the Politics of Transfiguration* [Berkeley and Los Angeles: University of California Press, 1988], p. 234).

79. This once prevalent view has, for the most part, lost its force in the philosophical community. Nonetheless, since some of Nietzsche's remarks do invite this unfortunate interpretation, it remains a view to be reckoned with.

achievements, art and philosophy, are thus to be explained in terms of the will to power.[80]

Now, instead of imagining brutes bashing each other, we are instructed to picture playwrights competing and philosophers arguing. These activities are simply more civilized forms of 'domination'.

Similarly, though not expressly set forth in terms of domination, Heidegger will claim that "the basic character of beings as such is 'will to power'."[81] Furthermore, the will to power turns out to be the 'will to will': the taking up of value simply for the sake of the power exercised in the taking. As we have already seen above, in this final form (the Übermensch) the will to will empties the world of significance; it appropriates and dominates for the sake of domination. "To will is to will-to-be-master."[82] As in Kaufmann's description, the will to power may assume many forms. However, these many forms will share an essential structure and essential goals: the will to will pursues a world in which things are efficient, articulate, ready for use, assimilable. In Heidegger's view, no form of the will to power can be benign in the manner of Kaufmann's artists and philosophers.

Different as these two visions are, they share some significant features. First, the will to power is seen as a force of domination, of appropriation, and the ways in which this domination can be expressed are vast, from the writing of dialogues to the waging of wars. In the case of Kaufmann, this view seems to collapse in on itself in much the same way as the 'trivial' view, inasmuch as every event, every act, can be redescribed as an act of 'domination', whether it be a painter 'dominating' a canvas or a general dominating a battlefield. Here again, the notion of 'domination' loses its explanatory force and becomes devoid of content. A second, more complicated, type of descriptive collapse is seen in Heidegger, who asserts that all the forms of will to will begin to resemble each other in their domination of the earth and its resources precisely because the reduction of the will to will's variety of expression is the essence of its metaphysical machinery.

Both these views, and indeed, all the views of the will to power considered thus far are *metaphysical*: they insist that there is an essence, a basic drive, a fundamental quality that is manifested in, or by, events and objects in the world. A metaphysical view must therefore assert that some thing,

80. Kaufmann, *Nietzsche: Philosopher, Psychologist, Antichrist* (Princeton: Princeton University Press, 1974), p. 192.

81. Heidegger, *Nietzsche: The Will to Power as Art*, vol. 1, p. 25.

82. Heidegger, "The Word of Nietzsche," p. 77.

called will to power, is true in all descriptions of the world, or true in all perspectives. Of course, this is precisely the metaphysical claim that Nietzsche rejects. If some drive, force, or metaphysical logic were true of every perspective, then we would have an 'essential' account of things: uninteresting, or uninformative, perhaps, but an objective view nonetheless. Indeed, Nietzsche does hold that a kind of objectivity exists, but not as a single, distilled appellation (namely, 'will to power').

> There is only a perspective seeing, only a perspective 'knowing'; and the more affects we allow to speak about one thing, the more eyes, different eyes, we can use to observe one thing, the more complete will our concept of this thing, our 'objectivity', be.[83]

Quite simply, Nietzsche's perspectivism, his insistence on the 'perspective optics of life', refuses all such essentialist accounts of the will to power.

In describing Nietzsche's attack on the 'Ding an sich', Alexander Nehamas makes this observation:

> A thing, (Nietzsche) insists, cannot be distinguished . . . from its various interrelations. Objects are conditioned by other objects through and through: " 'Things that have a constitution in themselves' — a dogmatic idea with which one must break absolutely" (*The Will to Power* 559). Construed in this manner, the will to power is not a general metaphysical or cosmological theory. On the contrary, it provides a reason why no general theory of the character of the world and the things that constitute it can ever be given.

The will to power is "an activity that . . . constitutes the character of everything in the world."[84] However, there is no discrete vantage point from which to observe this activity: only perspectives exist, each perspective with its own account of the world and the forces at work in it. Any attribution of will to power is bound to the perspective that generated it, and it cannot be sensibly extracted as the essence or 'law' of that perspective. Indeed, Nietzsche extends this 'uniqueness' to every act:

> Every action that has ever been done was done in an altogether unique and irretrievable way, and this will be equally true of every future

---

83. Nietzsche, *The Genealogy of Morals*, Essay III, 12.
84. Nehamas, *Nietzsche: Life as Literature*, p. 80.

> action; that all regulations about actions relate only to their coarse
> exterior . . . that these regulations may lead to some semblance of
> sameness, but really only to semblance; that as one contemplates or
> looks back upon any action at all, it is and remains impenetrable; that
> our opinions about 'good' and 'noble' and 'great' can never be proved
> true by our actions because every action is unknowable; that our
> opinions, valuations and tables of what is good certainly belong among
> the most powerful levers in the involved mechanism of our actions,
> but that in any particular case the law of their mechanism is unknow-
> able.[85]

The law is 'undemonstrable' not because there are no principles or powers
at work, but because its essential character cannot be captured by means
of such 'semblances'. The term 'will to power', as a generalizable principle
or law, is indeed such a semblance: in order to understand an act as 'will to
power' we must restrict our account to that act itself.

Finally, every identifiable instance of the will to power will have its own
'genealogy'; obviously, the cultural setting determines which sorts of will
to power can emerge and which cannot.[86] Both metaphysically and historically, we are warned against generalizations.

What, then, is the common element in Nietzsche's many attributions of
the will to power? The usual interpretive approach might be called 'external', since it examines the activities of will to power in a search for some
common feature. Recall the meaning of the previous passage from *The
Gay Science*: we should look away from the 'coarse exterior' of actions.
Instead, we might consider the 'experience' of certain activities; perhaps
there is a quality of a person's experience that can be called 'will to power'.
The term 'experience', however, is unfortunate in that it suggests some
sort of private, subjective experience of strength or power. 'Experience' is
meant to indicate the unfettered exercise of a person's energies, a kind of
effortless play. We may recall the child of "The Three Metamorphoses":

> The child is innocence and forgetfulness, a new beginning, a sport, a
> self-propelling wheel, a first motion, a sacred Yes . . . the spirit now

---

85. Nietzsche, *The Gay Science* 335.

86. Hubert Dreyfus has remarked that various ways of life are no longer possible because
the relevant context is missing (*Being-in-the-World: A Commentary on Heidegger's* Being
and Time, *Division I* [Cambridge, Mass.: MIT Press, 1991], p. 24). For example, a person can
no longer be a 'hero' as the Greeks could; a person can perform similar actions and make
similar claims, yet these actions and claims are senseless outside of the culture that created
them.

wills its own will, the spirit sundered from the world now wins its own world.[87]

This 'sport' is a moment of utter abandon, but it is not an 'experience of abandon' in the modern sense, which suggests a contrived and self-conscious effort at something. "The mountain hike was a great experience" implies that the person was focused on having a great experience, not on the hike itself. Such expressions make the un-Nietzschean division between the act and the experience of that act.

To remark that all forms of will to power denote a common experience is to point out a kind of affective quality in the individual. An act of will to power is one of potency, mastery, and freedom, characteristics more properly identified with the agent rather than the act (although this distinction must be provisional, since the boundary between 'agent' and 'act' is always drawn perspectivally). What kind of individual embodies will to power? Nietzsche's remarks about the child suggest that this individual will display an absorbed playfulness, a 'forgetfulness' that characterizes his behavior. This lack of self-consciousness can also be observed in persons engaged in an activity in which they are highly skilled.[88] This kind of 'forgetfulness' is thus not a species of mindlessness or childish behavior, but a supreme sort of self-realization; indeed, only the very skilled can become absorbed in their work or play in this manner.

This description of 'flow' may resemble Nietzsche's account of the 'child'. However, we might expand the notion of this lack of monitoring — a rather infrequent mental state — to a more general psychological characteristic. Someone may be 'unaware' of herself as a subject who acts or is acted upon because she is absorbed in the employment of her own powers, which is to say that her attention would not be focused on her powers as such, but on the ends she is effecting. 'Noble' types are often

---

87. Nietzsche, "Of the Three Metamorphoses," in *Thus Spake Zarathustra*.

88. Cf. Hubert Dreyfus and Stuart Dreyfus, *Mind Over Machine* (New York: The Free Press, 1986), p. 40:

> There are rare moments, however, when all monitoring ceases. We are referring to those brief periods of what is sometimes called 'flow', when performance, accompanied by a feeling of euphoria, reaches its peak. Athletes describe the phenomenon as playing 'out of your head' . . . 'flow' is not a . . . stage of the mental activities that produce skilled behavior but rather the cessation of the monitoring activity that normally accompanies the higher levels.

Cf. also Tracy B. Strong and his account of Nietzschean play in *Friedrich Nietzsche and the Politics of Transfiguration*, pp. 278-81.

'forgetful' or 'unaware' of their own powers in this way: the 'noble' person extends his powers to their limit, without bothering to take stock of the effects or consequences which that extension might entail. Nietzsche thus describes this 'noble' individual in the first essay of *The Genealogy of Morals*, section 10:

> It is a sign of strong, rich temperament that they cannot for long take seriously their enemies, their misfortunes, their misdeeds; for such characters have in them an excess of plastic curative power, and also a power of oblivion. (A good modern example of the latter is Mirabeau, who lacked all memory for insults and meannesses done to him, and who was unable to forgive because he had forgotten).

A similar observation is made in *The Gay Science* 55:

> The passion that attacks those who are noble is peculiar, and they fail to realize this. It involves the use of a rare and singular standard and almost a madness . . . the discovery of values for which no scales have been invented yet . . . a self-sufficiency that overflows and gives to men and things . . . it was rarity and a lack of awareness of this rarity that made a person noble . . .

This lack of self-consciousness creates its own kind of liberation. Although Nietzsche is generally skeptical about 'freedom', he will praise the noble spirit for this peculiar sort of freedom through mastery. Only many moments of self-mastery will produce a person so free in his response to the world.

> It will always be the mark of nobility that one feels no fear of oneself, expects nothing infamous of oneself, flies without scruple where we feel like flying, we freeborn birds. Wherever we may come there will always be freedom and sunlight around us.[89]

The 'will to power' displayed by the noble spirit, however, is not some 'internal' force that extrudes onto an objective scene. On the contrary, the context in which those powers are manifested is constitutive of what sort of *power* finally emerges.

---

89. Nietzsche, *The Gay Science* 294.

We can estimate our powers but not our power. Our circumstances do not only conceal and reveal it to us — no! they magnify and diminish it. One should regard oneself as a variable quantity whose capacity for achievement can under favorable circumstances perhaps equal the highest ever known: one should thus reflect on one's circumstances and spare no effort in observing them.[90]

Having offered this sketch of what the will to power is — namely, a kind of psychological affect, one characterized by potency and free, yet skillful, expression — we might pause and consider some possible objections. First, it might seem that this definition of will to power must include *any* unimpeded activity or venting of energies, from closing a door to composing a cantata.[91] If so, our account will, like earlier accounts, suffer from a serious sort of 'trivialization'. Consider, however, the following passage from *Daybreak* 500:

> *Against the grain.* — A thinker can for years on end force himself to think against the grain: that is to say, to pursue not the thoughts which offer themselves from within him but those to which an office, a prescribed schedule, an arbitrary kind of industriousness seem to oblige him. In the end, however, he will become sick: for this apparently moral overcoming of himself will ruin his nervous energy just as thoroughly as any regularly indulged in excess will do.

We would not characterize this thinker as displaying 'will to power', even though he is engaged in 'overcoming' himself (it is the *morality* of the overcoming that is apparent, not the overcoming itself); this thinker is a case of thwarted will to power. Not every exertion, not every activity will be will to power, for will to power entails freedom and 'loss of self', not self-conscious struggle with one's deepest inclinations. More important, this passage also illustrates why it is that 'external' accounts of the will to power can only rely on crude similarities; this scholar might seem, to those

---

90. Nietzsche, *Daybreak* 326.

91. In fact, this is precisely the sort of example that Randall Havas uses to describe Heidegger's account of the will to power: "Thus, as far as the essence of the will to power is concerned, there is no significant difference between the action of pulling a child out of the path of a moving car and, say, closing a gate" ("Nietzsche, Nihilism and the Autonomy of Reason: Nietzsche's Interpretation of the Will to Power" [Ph.D. diss., Harvard University, Cambridge, 1986]).

around him, to be fully exploring and using his powers. The will to power is a quality of the performance of the activity, not the activity itself.[92]

A second objection to our account is that of self-deception: a person may believe that they display will to power when in fact they merely suffer from a deluded sense of their own abilities. Certainly, Nietzsche is always interested in drawing the distinction between those who have power and those who crave power:

> Be sure you mark the difference: he who wants to acquire the feeling of power resorts to any means and disdains nothing that will nourish it. He who has it, however, has become very fastidious and noble in his tastes; he now finds few things satisfy him.[93]

In thinking about the deluded assertion of will to power, a pragmatic observation must be made: an individual who incessantly proclaims his power is probably not displaying the self-forgetfulness and absorption that characterize the will to power. Clearly, there will be no definitive test for will to power, for its 'proof' will lie within the account that is given of it, and, as I have already pointed out, there is no force called 'will to power' that can be extracted from a description of will to power. That is, in noting that an action displays will to power, we will be at the beginning of an interpretation of that action, which will be refined and altered as more interpretive pieces fall into place. The richer the interpretation — in other words, the more varied its elements are, including the person's own account of himself, those given by others, the person's upbringing, environment, and so forth — the more we may say about the attribution in question. This method is circular, but not viciously so. In fact, the procedure accords with Nietzsche's perspectivism, which we will discuss in the next chapter.

IV

A person's 'spiritual granite' is thus composed of 'accreted' value, values that can only be enumerated perspectivally. An obvious companionate

---

92. The frustrated thinker is intriguing in another aspect: he has a 'grain' that must be recognized and respected. This notion of an 'embedded' self, which can be glimpsed but cannot be radically altered, is a central issue of Chapter 2.

93. Nietzsche, *Daybreak* 48.

metaphor suggests itself: buried layers invite excavation. In fact, Nietzsche is committed to a kind of normative project; the 'good for persons' is an archaeological undertaking.

Here a constitutional observation must be distinguished from a normative one. Nietzsche claims that we are by 'nature' self-investigating. Again, this is a formal remark about our capacities that does not tell us what that investigating is like, or whether or not it is a 'life-affirming' behavior (clearly, given the range of Nietzsche's remarks about this capacity, it is clear that it can be healthful as well as harmful). Human creatures raise questions about themselves, but these questions can be self-deceived or motivated by *ressentiment*; the usefulness of the enterprise will ultimately turn on the spirit and the intentions of the investigator.

Nietzsche's most thorough account of his own archaeology is in *Daybreak*, a pursuit that is both scathingly honest and wholly private.

> In this book you will discover a 'subterranean man' at work, one who tunnels and mines and undermines. You will see him — presupposing you have eyes capable of seeing this work in the depths — going forward slowly, cautiously, gently inexorable . . . he who proceeds on his own path in this fashion encounters no one: that is inherent in 'proceeding on one's own path'. . . . For his path is his alone. . . . I tunnelled into the foundations, I commenced an investigation and digging out of an ancient faith, one upon which we philosophers have for a couple of millennia been accustomed to build as if upon the firmest of all foundations. . . . I commenced to undermine our faith in morality.[94]

Nietzsche's investigation is twofold: he is digging up the evaluative material that he himself is composed of, but in so doing he inevitably unearths and, in some cases, undermines parts of the moral sediment that constitutes the culture at large. There is no reliable way to cordon off Nietzsche's examination of himself from his attack on the moral antecedents of his society. Nietzsche considers himself made of these materials, yet his personal account of them necessarily shapes a critique of the moral history of the West. His dig, however, does not simply uncover moral strata common to everyone. It reveals uniquely Nietzschean features of the moral terrain at the same time as it disturbs and alters those shared moral accretions. Nietzsche well understands that his reflections on his own moral material could have a disturbing effect on the moral ground we all share.

---

94. Ibid., preface, sections 1, 2.

At this point the metaphor of 'archaeology' becomes seriously mixed, because Nietzsche will treat those ancient moral materials as something we 'inherit' and bear within ourselves. The history of our moral feelings is 'genealogical' as well as 'archaeological': our feelings in moral matters are 'inherited' and constitute our 'instincts'. We may leave aside this metaphorical tangle for a moment, and simply follow Nietzsche's own curious and revealing use of these terms.

Nietzsche as archaeologist offers two responses to the material he uncovers. First, he is typically skeptical about his finds; he calls into question not only the sense of the value itself, but its motives, origins, and history. These skeptical inquiries usually reveal a host of incompatible claims and historical lacunae, so that a kind of philosophical creativity is called for. Such an epistemological undertaking is familiar to the professional anthropologist: what does this shard of pottery, this tile or bead, mean? The question "What is it?" can, in many cases, never be completely settled, and this indeterminacy requires the archaeologist to be fluid and responsive in his investigating. By calling into question the received account of how a particular value was established, the sense of the moral object itself is also altered. The disruption of one moral account may well bring a wholly different set of evaluations into view.

The second important feature of the Nietzschean dig is often overlooked by readers who are taken with the sheer destructiveness of his remarks. Nietzsche cautions himself (and his readers) to be mindful of the potency of these ancient artifacts. They are potent because of their antiquity: the 'deeper' they are located in our moral history, the more of our moral life 'rests' on them. They are also powerful, however, because they live on (in many cases only a half-life) in our current moral sensibilities. We are taught to provide arguments for our moral behavior, but we 'inherit' our moral instincts, which is to say that we unreflectively absorb a host of moral responses long before we have the wherewithal to think about them: "Thoughts are not inherited, only feelings."[95] Futhermore, Nietzsche insists that the magnitude and weight of our moral instincts — however confused and obscure — are far more powerful than the reflective powers we bring to bear on them.

> It is clear that the moral feelings are transmitted in this way: children observe in adults inclinations for and aversions to certain actions and, as born apes, imitate these inclinations and aversions; in later life they

---

95. Ibid., 30.

find themselves full of these acquired and well-exercised affects and consider it only decent to try to account for and justify them. . . . To this extent the history of moral feelings is quite different from the history of moral concepts. The former are powerful before the action, the latter especially after the action in face of the need to pronounce upon it.[96]

Moral reasoning is thus reduced to a kind of intellectual mending. The disparate pieces of our heritage must be made to fit together, a demand generated by the power of custom itself.[97] But is the weight of this inheritance a boon or an impediment? Should we be grateful to have discovered these largely intractable values in ourselves, or should we attempt to dismantle this moral material?

Nietzsche typically champions the thinker's own reflective vitality and resourcefulness.

'Trust your feelings!' — But feelings are nothing final or original; behind feelings there stand judgments and evaluations which we inherit in the form of feelings (inclinations, aversions). The inspiration born of a feeling is the grandchild of a judgment — and often of a false judgment! — and in any event not a child of your own. To trust one's feelings — means to give more obedience to one's grandfather and grandmother and their grandparents than to the gods which are in us: our reason and our experience.[98]

Despite his skeptical commitment to 'undermining' this heritage, however, Nietzsche is ambivalent in his view. He is not recommending the wholesale destruction of our moral legacy (and the reasons for this are the subject of the next chapter). Some things uncovered in the excavation must be rooted out; others will be beautiful, valuable, and well worth modifying for our own modern (and indeed postmodern) purposes. No absolute basis for deliberating about what we keep and what we discard is available; choices at the dig site are difficult, often painful, and ultimately provisional, perspectival.

Even if the decisions we make about our 'inheritance' are ill-informed and subject to change, our struggle to understand our moral constitution is good for us, and in two ways: it exercises our capacity for self-

---

96. Ibid., 34.
97. Ibid., 9 and 16.
98. Ibid., 35; see also 81 and 99.

investigation, and since it does so, our 'digging' is, surprisingly, a 'moral' activity. "In this book faith in morality is withdrawn — but why? Out of morality!"[99] Nietzsche's investigation is 'moral' because it is generated by a profound human characteristic, and, more important, because it honors the impossibility of absolutely answering the questions so raised.

Having considered the archaeological process, we may now ask: why does Nietzsche insist on mixing his metaphors? Why introduce a genealogical trope into a work that is announced as an archaeological project? A first thought is that Nietzsche needs to remind us that we are composed of both 'live' and 'dead' material; some of what we uncover is fossilized, a remnant of life captured 'in amber' and will merely be the occasion for curiosity or derision, but nothing more.[100] The metaphor of archaeology, however, is deeply misleading if we understand ourselves to be distinct from the dig site: we cannot simply put down our tools and go home. The 'dig' takes place in common cultural ground, and it reveals moral behaviors that still exist, quotidian and often unseen, in our lives. Hence, the importance of 'genealogy'. Atavistic remnants of ancient human practices are alive in our bodies and behaviors.

The obvious philosophical descendant of this complex of images is Michel Foucault. Both 'archaeology' and genealogy' are crucial images in his descriptions of his work. Foucault's project is usually understood as 'archeological' at the outset, becoming 'genealogical' as it matures. 'Archaeology' is a search for rules that structure a particular discourse, or a 'grammar'.

> If one wishes to undertake an archaeological analysis of knowledge itself, it is not these celebrated controversies that ought to be used as the guidelines and articulation of such a project. One must reconstitute the general system of thought whose network, in its positivity, renders an interplay of simultaneous and apparently contradictory opinions possible. *It is this network that defines the conditions that make a controversy or problem possible, and that bears the historicity of knowledge.*[101]

Foucault the archaeologist is not interested as such in the arcane history of various philosophical squabbles; rather, he wants to reveal what makes

---

99. Ibid., preface, 4.

100. Nietzsche, *Human, All Too Human* 208.

101. Foucault, *The Order of Things: An Archaeology of the Human Sciences* (New York: Random House, 1970), p. 75; emphasis mine.

a particular set of disagreements possible. Both 'speaker' and 'meaning' are externally constructed; archaeology uncovers these linguistic structures.

So described, Foucault's project seems very much in the structuralist tradition, a label Foucault furiously denies in the forward to the English edition of *Les Mots et Les Choses*. But some similarities with structuralist practice are well worth considering. First of all, the object of interest is not a meaning-giving subject, but a linguistic structure that creates a certain kind of subject. Furthermore, regularities characterize discourse, and these regularities may be seen as an 'interpretive grid' or 'system'.

Foucault's work after *The Archaeology of Knowledge* is described as 'genealogical', which means (roughly) that it provides an account of how it is that particular values (and sets of values) emerge from the complex relations of truth and power. Genealogy, like archaeology, is also in the business of revealing what constitutes a culture, yet the account it provides is both historical and subversive. Genealogy is an alternative history, offering a different view of the intentions and desires that fueled various intellectual and moral controversies. Obviously, such an account will need to interpret what it is that is upheld as truth, and what presents itself as powerful, and why. A genealogical study must uncover the sordid truths that lurk on the culture's margins and give an account of their power, and, perhaps more important, why these truths were historically suppressed or distorted. Genealogy, in its survey of cultural materials, *must* evaluate and interpret, providing both a new understanding of what seem to be self-evident cultural antecedents as well as standing in judgment of those antecedents.

In their account of Foucault's methods, Dreyfus and Rabinow argue that Foucault preserves the best of both structuralist and hermeneutic techniques. Foucault's archaeology reveals how language structures both subjects and objects while denying that this 'grammar' is composed of meaningless elements. His genealogy is 'hermeneutic' in its effort to reveal hidden complexes of truth and power, yet this account is not set forth as an objective rendering of hidden motives and desires.[102] Dreyfus and Rabinow also claim that Foucault moves away from archaeological practice and becomes more interested in providing a reading of various cultural forces. This developmental view of Foucault's work has been much argued, and indeed Foucault is himself not interested in settling the question:

---

102. Hubert Dreyfus and Paul Rabinow, *Michel Foucault: Beyond Structuralism and Hermeneutics* (Chicago: University of Chicago Press, 1983), pp. xxiii, xxiv.

his remarks on this controversy are often obscure and inconsistent. Michael Mahon's insightful review of these distinctions cites a 1983 interview with Martin Jay:

> What I mean by archaeology is a methodological framework for my analysis. What I mean by genealogy is both the reason and the target of analyzing those discourses as events, and what I am trying to show is how those discursive events have determined in a certain way what constitutes ourselves . . . the genealogy is the finality of the analysis, and the archaeology is the material and methodological framework.[103]

Archaeology is the method, and genealogy is the goal. The 'dig' provides us with the means, yet the account given of those means is the purpose of the work. The parsing of Foucault's project is not the main point here, however. If we consider the difference between these two endeavors, some worthwhile comparisons with Nietzsche appear. In *The Order of Things*, Foucault tells a rather Nietzschean tale about archaeological work:

> It is in this sense that archaeology can give an account of the existence of a general grammar, a natural history, and an analysis of wealth, and thus open up a free, undivided area in which the history of the sciences, the history of ideas, and the history of opinions can, if they wish, frolic with ease.[104]

Archaeology provides a structure for a kind of interpretive, genealogical play. "One is led therefore to the project of a *pure description of discursive events* as the horizon for the search for the unities that form within it."[105]

An analogous, though by no means obvious or systematic, split can be seen in Nietzsche's writings. On the one hand, Nietzsche is interested in what it is that makes certain philosophical puzzles and conflicts possible. At such moments Nietzsche is focused on the values that structure a subject's view of him- or herself. In these passages human individuals are no more than passive receptacles for cultural powers seriously beyond their reckoning. On the other hand, Nietzsche, the master interpreter and

---

103. Michael Mahon, *Foucault's Nietzschean Genealogy: Truth, Power and the Subject* (Albany: State University of New York Press, 1992), p. 105.

104. Foucault, *The Order of Things*, p. 208.

105. Foucault, *The Archaeology of Knowledge and The Discourse on Language*, trans. A. M. Sheridan Smith (New York: Pantheon Books, 1972), p. 27.

genealogist, is always interested in an *active* account of how our values have been shaped and mis-shaped, the hidden desires and intentions at work in what seem to be benign and ordinary reflections. A constant play and exchange is at work in the corpus: Nietzsche wants to show his (careful) reader what it is that constitutes her or him *while at the same time* revealing what we thinkers (free spirits and others) have done to that inherited material with our creative and skeptical powers. And, of course, the latter interpretive activity is meant to be a kind of 'frolic'. It must be playful (and indeed 'fröhliche') because there will be no final, authoritative version of why we have taken up certain values in the way that we have, and, moreover, no absolute catalogue of what those values are. Nietzsche the archaeologist will uncover what we are made of, while Nietzsche the genealogist will compose a story about those materials and their interrelated powers and truth claims. Sometimes the genealogy necessarily disturbs our sense of those prior materials—was the initial account of those prior elements sufficient?—and thus the dig begins again. It makes little sense to look for hard distinctions here. These ways of thinking about human history are, in Nietzsche's writings, not thematically discrete.

Here we see a serious disanalogy with Foucault's use of these metaphors, for Foucault does intend us to understand his archaeological remarks as distinct and different from his genealogical ones.

Nietzsche, as I have argued, is investigating 'value', but value, as we have seen, is a loaded term, open to misunderstanding and abuse. In some cases Nietzsche means 'cultural commonplaces', highly articulated and well-worn moral observations of daily life. At other times he means something like 'cultural forces' that are neither usually reflected on nor easily available for scrutiny, such as our ordinary remarks about causation or 'subjects' and 'objects'. Nietzsche often investigates these 'constitutive' values through a dismantling of 'articulate' value. We might be tempted, then, to think that a rough analogy obtains between Nietzsche's work and Foucault's work. 'Constitutive values' are like Foucault's set of 'discursive conditions', while the unities that emerge in the 'interstices' of these conditions are isomorphic with Nietzsche's 'articulate' values. Furthermore, these levels demand different strategies: archaeology reveals these discursive conditions, while genealogy as an interpretive gambit both reveals and creates the unities therein.

This comparison fails, however, to acknowledge Nietzsche's refusal to distinguish firmly between 'articulate' and 'constitutive' value. Foucault certainly differentiates his structural remarks from his interpretive ones; Nietzsche denies any such distinctions. At some moments Nietzsche will take great pains to reveal to his reader what was previously treated as a truism about human life. For example (and indeed examples of this classificatory slipperiness abound), in *Daybreak* 97 the slavishness of human nature is merely assumed in order to make a point about moral behavior, while in section 101 Nietzsche labors to uncover our slavishness and then display it to us. That which is hidden and inchoate seriously depends on what we are investigating and why (an important point that we will return to later). Wittgenstein's comment about the 'hardening' of propositions indicates a comparable indeterminacy:

> It might be imagined that some propositions, of the form of empirical propositions, were hardened and functioned as channels for such empirical propositions as were not hardened but fluid; and that this relation altered with time, in that fluid propositions hardened, and hard ones became fluid . . . the river-bed of thoughts may shift. But I distinguish between the movement of the waters on the river-bed and the shift of the bed itself; *though there is not a sharp division of the one from the other.*[106]

For both Nietzsche and Foucault, there are two 'levels' of material, and two responses to that material. In each case there is an 'uncovering', a digging up of constitutive material, and corresponding interpretations within those structures. Nietzsche, however, refuses to define absolutely what it is he is working on, and, moreover, how best to deal with it. Here a deeper reason for Nietzsche's conflation of tropes is found: he does so because he disallows any rule that dictates where one sort of material, and thus one sort of strategy, leaves off and another begins. It is truly a matter of perspective. In one light a particular set of values will be seen in high relief, while another sort of investigation may well eclipse those values. Tracing (and perforce creating) a lineage may indeed, at some moments, become the excavation of a cultural artifact. One sort of enterprise shades into the other, and we can only distinguish them provisionally.

But these remarks only serve to press the question more firmly upon us: what is a 'perspective', and what is it to say that values both emerge from and make up our perspectives?

---

106. Ludwig Wittgenstein, *On Certainty*, trans. Denis Paul and G. E. M. Anscombe (New York: Harper Torchbooks, 1969), sections 96–97; emphasis mine.

2

Epistemology

the 'land' and the 'sea'

A tedium saddened by cruel hopes still believes in the last fare-
well of handkerchiefs! And perhaps the masts, inviting storms,
are among those that a gale bends above wrecks that are lost,
without masts, without masts or fertile islands. . . . But, O
my heart, listen to the sailor's song!

— Mallarmé, *Brise Marine*

The archaeological process, the in-
vestigation of our inheritance, is fueled by reflection. Although Nietzsche
investigates a variety of human behaviors it is only this act of investigating
that consistently manages to hold his interest. At times Nietzsche seems to
regard critical thinking (or, at the least, a healthy suspicion) as something
much like an end in itself. A relentless, critical scrutiny is the means of
reaching an adequate conclusion as well as being every conclusion's tire-
less companion; suspicion becomes the apostate's article of 'anti-faith'.

> If this book is pessimistic even into the realm of morality, even to the
> point of going beyond faith in morality. . . . For it does in fact exhibit a
> contradiction and is not afraid of it: in this book faith in morality is
> withdrawn — but why? Out of morality! . . . there is no doubt that a
> 'thou shalt' still speaks to us too, we still obey a stern law set over
> us . . . we too are still men of conscience . . . namely, in that we do
> not want to return to that which we consider outlived and decayed, to
> anything 'unworthy of belief', be it called God, virtue, truth, justice,
> charity . . . we are hostile from the heart . . . to every kind of faith.[1]

NO FAITH!

No principle, cause, or judgment — in short, no value — will be regarded as
above suspicion. We are called to reflect on our moral assumptions.
  The power of reflection to critique, alter, or overthrow accepted con-

---

1. Nietzsche, *Daybreak*, preface.

clusions is a central issue in all of Nietzsche's writings. Reflection is treated either as an 'implement' designed to effect the intended alteration, or — and this is perhaps the deeper point — as itself the phenomenon to be examined. It is helpful to review the scope of Nietzsche's 'stands on reflection'. The following collection of passages represents a sample of Nietzsche's many attitudes toward the reflective process. Reflection is the surgical procedure that will excise our moral self-deceptions and illusions:

> The present condition of one . . . science has made necessary the awakening of moral observation, and mankind cannot be spared the horrible sight of the psychological operating table, with its knives and forceps. For now that science rules which asks after the origin and history of moral feelings . . . the old philosophy doesn't even acknowledge such problems and has always used meager excuses to avoid investigating the origin . . . of moral feelings.[2]

An older, less optimistic Nietzsche predicts the erosion of belief caused by reflection:

> The greatest recent event — that 'God is dead', that the belief in the Christian God is becoming unbelieveable — is already beginning to cast its first shadows over Europe . . . and how much must collapse now that this faith has been undermined . . . for example, the whole of our European morality.[3]

Reflection is not only the harbinger of our cultural fate; the reflective state can also be an intensely personal exercise in self-examination. The demon's proposition is an invitation to reflect in this manner:

> What if some day or night a demon were to steal after you into your loneliest loneliness and say to you: 'This life as you live it and have lived it, you will have to live once more and innumerable times more. . . . Would you not throw yourself down and gnash your teeth and curse the demon who spoke thus? . . . If this thought gained possession of you it would change you as you are or perhaps crush you.[4]

---

2. Nietzsche, *Human, All Too Human* 37.
3. Nietzsche, *The Gay Science* 343.
4. Ibid., 341.

And, of course, Nietzsche's infamous 'doing philosophy with a hammer' is the relentless analysis of our most sacred philosophical notions:

> This little book is a grand declaration of war; and as regards the sounding-out of idols, this time they are not idols of the age but eternal idols which are here touched with the hammer as with a tuning fork.[5]

Nietzsche is more interested in the reflective *attack* than in the reflective establishment of any set of principles; indeed, it is this sort of 'hyper-reflectivity' that Heidegger deems responsible for the most pernicious form of nihilism. Recall that Heidegger understands the Übermensch to be the paradigmatic reflector, a person who takes up particular values and practices merely in order to critically dismantle them. If we regard Heidegger's account as an unacceptable rendering of the Übermensch, then our task is to explain Nietzschean reflectivity as a non-nihilistic activity, one that manages to do its dismantling work while still allowing us to inhabit particular 'ways of life' (and to explain how it is that any evaluations have managed to resist the reflective process).[6]

---

5. Nietzsche, *The Twilight of the Idols*, preface.

6. Critical accounts of Heidegger's later works will claim that Heidegger really does *not* see the Übermensch as essentially characterized by reflection. The Übermensch 'outgrows' a succession of evaluations, a sort of development that is not *itself* necessarily a reflective activity. Heidegger's view of the Übermensch is a complicated matter; still, the preceding claim must be briefly addressed here. In volume 4 of the Nietzsche lectures, Heidegger remarks, "Nietzsche . . . stakes everything on the priority of man as subject" (*Nietzsche, Volume 4, Nihilism*, ed. Krell, p. 130). Here Heidegger is asserting that Nietzsche is still recognizably Cartesian, despite all the evidence to the contrary. Nietzsche's 'subject' is the one who 'represents' in order to 'overcome' that representation, in other words, the nihilistic overcoming of the will to will. Heidegger then goes on to insist that this reflecting, positing, representing, and so forth, is not something that the subject does; rather, that is what the subject *is*. This positing 'constitution' is meant to explain why Nietzsche's philosophy is a philosophy 'of the body'. "The body is to be placed first 'methodologically'." Nonetheless, Heidegger concludes that "Nietzsche posits the body in place of the soul and consciousness alters nothing in the fundamental metaphysical position which is determined by Descartes" (p. 133). The problem, I take it, is that the Übermensch is essentially a 'subject' whose world is composed of 'representations'. Even if the *way* in which the mechanism of self-overcoming works is not primarily a reflective one (for example, the Übermensch just asserts his powers, just explores various activities, and it *turns out* that his assertions are representations), *the problem is still our reflective capacity*, which is the origin of those representations. When I remark that Heidegger objects to, for example, the 'reflective' quality of the Übermensch, that statement is an abbreviation of the reflective dilemma that the 'overcomings' of the Übermensch represent, not an account of how it is that the Übermensch goes about 'overcoming' his values (although his activity must surely be reflective to a large degree).

One way to begin that explanation is to examine Nietzsche's customary *NOTE* epistemological trope. Of the many images Nietzsche uses to describe our coming to know the world, the most compelling and persistent is that of the voyager at sea. The notion of 'being at sea' is delightfully ambiguous. It suggests not only the explorer's daring but the confusion, the becalming, that can blight an intellectual search. Zarathustra certainly makes much of this dual sense. As the paradigmatic voyager (at the end of the book Zarathustra is again off on another journey), he admires "cunning sails upon dreadful seas,"[7] and despite his claim that "like a sail . . . my wisdom fares over the sea,"[8] he fears what might be discovered: "There stands the boat: over there perhaps the way to the great Nothingness!"[9]

There are two senses in which 'being at sea' is metaphorically significant. First, our attention is called to the constantly shifting horizon. A person on the water, even when stationary, is constantly aware of her relation as viewer to what is seen: as the ship moves what is seen, what can be seen, moves as well. The connection between the trope of the sea and that of vision is important; on the water the land-dweller's visual habits are self-consciously altered. Of course, this initially self-conscious seeing, this awareness of seeing from a particular, perhaps temporary, point-of-view, is part of Nietzsche's account of perspectivism (of which more in a moment).

The loss of solid ground is a second important feature of being at sea. The sailor knows that he depends on his ship for survival, that it is frail and tiny in comparison to the ocean it traverses; hence, at times, a longing for the assurance and stability, the un-self-conscious behaviors of those who live on the land. This loss of ground is felt most keenly in moral concerns. The person who calls her values into question ultimately wants to make solid claims about her moral practices, but that very 'voyaging', the reflective process she has embarked upon, has destroyed the ground she once inhabited.

> *In the horizon of the infinite.* — We have left the land and have embarked. We have burned our bridges behind us — indeed, we have gone farther and destroyed the land behind us. Now, little ship, look out! Beside you is the ocean, and at times it lies spread out like silk and gold and reveries of graciousness. But hours will come when you will

7. Nietzsche, "Of the Vision and the Riddle," in *Thus Spoke Zarathustra,* Part 3. The same passage appears in "Why I Write Such Excellent Books," in *Ecce Homo.*

8. Nietzsche, "Of the Famous Philosophers," in *Thus Spoke Zarathustra*, Part 2.

9. Nietzsche, "Of Old And New Law Tables," in *Thus Spoke Zarathustra*, Part 3.

realize that it is infinite and that there is nothing more awesome than infinity. Oh, the poor bird that felt free and now strikes the walls of this cage! Woe, when you feel homesick for the land as if it had offered more freedom — and there is no longer any 'land'.

The 'land' is, of course, our moral tradition, and the very stuff that the archaeologist goes to work on. Here, however, a difference between the ontological and epistemological sense of this metaphor is apparent. The ontological remark that we are composed of accreted value — value that is nonetheless vulnerable to the skeptic's assault — is less disturbing than the epistemological image of the utter destruction of these values (with the exception of the remnants of tradition preserved in the vessel itself) and our subsequent sea voyage. The ontological metaphor suggests a permanence and sturdiness that the epistemological one does not: we are reassured that no amount of digging will absolutely destroy our common ground.

The image of digging is also, perhaps, suggestive of refinement: we will discard what is outmoded, useless, cumbersome, and leave the rest. Certainly, many of Nietzsche's own examples imply this refining process; for example, *Daybreak* 16:

> Among barbarous peoples there exists a species of customs whose purpose appears to be custom in general: minute and fundamentally superfluous stipulations (as for example those among the Kamshadales forbidding the scraping of snow from the shoe with a knife, the impaling of coal on a knife, the placing of an iron in the fire — and he who contravenes them meets death!) which, however, keep continually in the consciousness the constant proximity of custom, the perpetual compulsion to practice customs: so as to strengthen the mighty proposition with which civilization begins: any custom is better than no custom.

The passage seems to suggest that those who inherit these practices will, on reflection, ultimately discard these irrational habits.

A prosaic illustration of such investigating helps to raise some questions about the assumption that we can simply discard what is no longer relevant. (Appropriately enough, it is rather outmoded in terms of gender.) A mother is teaching her daughter how to cook a pot roast; she tells her that she must cut off one end of the roast before putting it in the pan. The daughter asks her why this step is necessary. Does it tenderize the meat? Regulate the temperature? The mother admits that she doesn't know why she removes the end of the roast, and in due course the grandmother is consulted, who tells them that *she* cut off the end because her pan was not big enough.

This tale, while hardly as dramatic as Nietzsche's own historical examples, does reveal one expectation that attaches to skeptical inquiry. The daughter is now free of a useless piece of behavior; now that she knows the origin of this ritual she understands that it is just that, a ritual detached from its initial sense and intent. The practice of pot roast cooking stays in place, but the process has been refined, improved, by her question.

The difficulty is that our ethical behaviors usually prompt a different sort of question, one that demands a primary, rather than subsidiary, account. Nietzsche's own examples of such questions, particularly in *Daybreak*, generally do not distinguish between questions about grounds and those that leave the practice more or less in place. A primary question wants to know about the basis of a behavior, while a subsidiary question is concerned with details of the behavior itself. A member of the Kamshadales may question the complex set of rules that attach to their use of iron implements, but *that* question, even if the origin is revealed as archaic or irrelevant, will not necessarily undo the practice (it will undo particular details of the practice). So too in the case of the pot roast: the daughter may stop cutting off the end of the meat but the practice of eating pot roast stays in place.

The truly disturbing question, and one we can well imagine being posed, is: why eat roasted meat? An investigation of this behavior may reveal that we have good reason to abandon this gustatory habit. A heightened awareness of the animals' suffering awakens our disgust; our improved nutritional knowledge tells us to eat differently; a better understanding of the waste and damage to the environment involved in raising cattle undoubtedly calls the practice of eating beef into question. But *this* instance of questioning a habit is puzzling: unlike a question that is concerned with refining a practice, where the appropriate response is clear (that is, it is hard to imagine the daughter stubbornly continuing to trim the roast), the outcome of this kind of questioning is impossible to predict. A person might be persuaded that eating beef is a ridiculous, indulgent habit that only serves the interests of the cattle industry, and thus give it up. Another may well see the force of these arguments and yet continue to eat meat (a different case from the person who simply owns up to being ridiculous and indulgent). What indeed *is* the status of these persistent habits, rituals, and practices? Why is it that some survive our primary questions, often flying in the face of what we have good reason to do, while others simply disappear? Are these inherited behaviors a kind of knowledge, and if so, what does it mean that they can so readily go out of existence in some cases, yet complacently remain in others?

In *Ethics and the Limits of Philosophy* Bernard Williams asks a similar question about the status of traditional ethical practice: do such practices constitute a body of knowledge? Williams uses an imaginary society that is 'minimally reflective' and 'maximally homogeneous', which he dubs the 'hypertraditional' society, as the test case for ethical knowledge. Specifically, do the members of this society display ethical knowledge when they make judgments according to their ethical concepts?

Our outlook on ethical behavior will determine our attitude toward this issue. Williams claims that there are two such outlooks, 'objectivist' and 'nonobjectivist'. In the objectivist model of ethical practice, Williams states,

> We shall see the members of the society as trying, in their local way, to find out the truth about values, an activity in which we and other human beings, and perhaps creatures who are not human beings, are engaged. We shall then see their judgments as having these general implications, rather as we see primitive statements about the stars as having implications that can be contradicted by more sophisticated statements about the stars.[10]

These ethical judgments are thus treated as having implications that far outstrip their actual use. Even though the members of the society do not see themselves as pressing toward the 'true ethical system' — certainly, they have not reflected on their ethical judgments in that way at all — an objectivist insistence that their judgments do in fact have this implication (and that their judgments fall short of the mark) is of course one of the ways in which reflection can destroy a traditional practice.[11]

The alternative model is 'nonobjectivist'. The nonobjectivist view does not consider traditional ethical judgments to have such general implications; thus, the failure of these practices to survive reflective scrutiny need not impugn the (potential) status of their judgments as knowledge, since the locals were never covertly making such universal claims in the first place. Instead, we can see the locals as possessing a knowledge of their

---

10. Bernard Williams, *Ethics and the Limits of Philosophy* (Cambridge: Harvard University Press, 1985), p. 147.

11. Of course, this is not a destruction of knowledge. By the lights of the objectivist view, there can only be false belief holding these practices in place, which is precisely what reflection reveals to us.

particular social world, a knowledge that, with the advent of reflection, is now defunct.[12]

The appeal of the nonobjectivist account is clear: traditional beliefs certainly seem to behave like a 'species' of knowledge, and the nonobjectivist can give the concepts employed in traditional judgment the appropriate 'epistemic credit'. Certainly, when ethical practices are abstractly conceived of and reflected on, principles of reflection become the standard against which they are measured. However, ethical practices do not necessarily fail to be knowledge in any form just because they fail to be knowledge at that reflective level. To suppose so, the nonobjectivist will claim, misunderstands the nature of ethical practices. If we return the concepts used by the locals to the social world that they shape and are shaped by, it is clear that the use of such concepts could well constitute knowledge the user had of that social world: not knowledge that these are the right concepts to use, for that would be knowledge at the level of reflection, but knowledge of situations picked out by those concepts within that world.

The disturbing result of the nonobjectivist view of ethical practice is that reflection can destroy ethical knowledge.

> If we accept that there can be knowledge at the hypertraditional or unreflective level; if we accept the obvious truth that reflection characteristically disturbs, unseats or replaces those traditional concepts; and if we agree that, at least as things are, the reflective level is not in a position to give us knowledge we did not have before — then we reach the notably un-Socratic conclusion that, in ethics, reflection can destroy knowledge.[13]

Is this conclusion one that Nietzsche endorses? We should note that Nietzsche's critique of morality is relentlessly 'objectivist' in its outlook. Nietzsche insists that moral claims *do* take themselves to be articulating

---

12. This sketch of the nonobjectivist position is not meant to suggest an implicit relativism. Williams remarks, "Even if there is no way in which divergent ethical beliefs can be brought to converge by independent inquiry or rational argument, this fact will not imply relativism. Each outlook may still be making claims it intends to apply to the whole world, not to just that part of it which is its 'own' world" (*Ethics and the Limits of Philosophy*, p. 159).

13. Ibid., p. 148. It is important to clarify what the phrase 'reflection destroys knowledge' is supposed to tell us. Reflection, Williams asserts, typically destroys traditional ethical practices. The question is whether or not the notions used in carrying out these traditional practices constitutes a kind of knowledge.

fundamental truths, and that a rigorous skepticism can reveal these claims to be false.

> 'To deny morality' — this can mean, first: to deny that the moral motives which men claim have inspired their actions have really done so. . . . Then it can mean: to deny that moral judgments are based on truths. Here it is admitted that they really are motives of action, but that in this way it is errors which, as the basis of all moral judgment, impel men to their moral actions. This is my point of view. . . . I also deny immorality: not that countless people feel themselves to be immoral, but that there is any true reason so to feel.[14]

Individuals are 'impelled' to their moral behavior by what they take to be moral truths. That, according to Nietzsche, is the devastating error, because by revealing moral dicta to be (at the very least) neither true nor false, the ground for action, namely, the truth of those views, has been removed.

Given this objectivist inclination, we may expect Nietzsche's remarks about social institutions to follow suit.

> Sometimes to act against one's better judgment when it comes to questions of custom: to give way in practice while keeping one's judgments to oneself; to do as everyone does and thus to show them consideration as it were in compensation for our deviant opinions: —  many tolerably free-minded people regard this, not merely as unobjectionable, but as 'honest', 'humane', 'tolerant', 'not being pedantic', and whatever else . . . with which the intellectual conscience is lulled to sleep . . . and thus this person takes his child for Christian baptism though he is an atheist . . . and (another) marries his wife in a church because her relatives are pious and is not ashamed to repeat vows before a priest. 'It doesn't really matter if people like us also do what everyone else does and has done' — this is the thoughtless prejudice! . . . For nothing matters more than that an already mighty, anciently established and irrationally recognized custom should be once more . . . confirmed as rational. . . . All respect to your opinions! But *little deviant acts* are worth more![15]

---

14. Nietzsche, *Daybreak* 103.
15. Ibid., 149.

Once again we see Nietzsche's fascination with skepticism and the behavior it can prompt. Raising questions about local customs through rebellion, 'little deviant acts', is worthier than the preservation of the concepts that establish particular practices. Nietzsche's interest in subversive acts of reflection does not leave much space for the stasis of traditional behavior. Despite his objectivist emphasis, however, he draws a conclusion that anticipates Williams's concerns. First, whatever it is that ethical concepts are, they are misunderstood when treated as pieces of propositional knowledge; second, just because they do not constitute that sort of knowledge does not mean that we therefore have no reason to act — or refrain from acting — in various ways. Consider the conclusion to the passage previously quoted from *Daybreak* 103:

> It goes without saying that I do not deny — unless I am a fool — that many actions called immoral ought to be avoided and resisted, or that many called moral ought to be done and encouraged — but I think the one should be encouraged and the other avoided *for other reasons than hitherto*.

These 'other reasons' are tantalizing. Here, evidently, is our best hope for a non-nihilistic account of Nietzsche's moral assault. Nietzsche claims that some behaviors should be preserved, but not the moral reasoning that accompanies them. What, then, will these 'other reasons' be like? What kind of support can they provide for our ethical behaviors, given that the usual sort of moral reason is susceptible to the reflective onslaught? On the other hand, are these new reasons simply a chimera? Is Karsten Harries right when he remarks that Nietzsche's destruction "leaves us no place to stand . . . Nietzsche now appears as a mad discoverer who, dreaming of a lost continent beneath the waves, begins to break apart the planks of his ship"?[16]

Before attempting a positive characterization of Nietzsche's alternative, however, another conceptual piece of the Nietzsche lexicon needs to be put in place; once again we must redirect our thinking. Nietzsche may praise the reflective 'hammer', but he also reminds us that the consequences of the hammer's blows are entirely a matter of one's *perspective*. Nietzsche's 'doctrine' of perspectivism can be seen as the necessary corollary to his commitment to skepticism.

In focusing on the power of reflection to destroy the use of ethical

---

16. Karsten Harries, "The Philosopher at Sea," in *Nietzsche's New Seas*, ed. Michael Gillespie and Tracy Strong (Chicago: University of Chicago Press, 1988), p. 43.

concepts we have only seen half of the account that Nietzsche provides. Certainly, reflection is a force able to 'unmask', 'unveil', or 'illuminate' that which was previously taken for granted. *But Nietzsche will insist that its revelatory force does not come from the void.* Reflection, according to Nietzsche, always emerges from a particular perspective, with built-in expectations, assumptions, and selectively collected facts. The claim is that perspectivism is the neglected amendment to an overweening reflective capacity. I need to say something first, however, about perspectivism as such.

II

Nietzsche's remarks about perspectives are quite difficult to explain (as well as being, for the most part, philosophically divisive and inflammatory), but some guidelines can be found. First of all, 'perspectivism' is not the same as 'relativism', although it could be considered a complex and sophisticated version of relativism. Nietzsche himself finds the views of relativists to be hopelessly puerile.

> They (historians of morality) . . . affirm some consensus . . . concerning certain principles of morals, and then they infer from this that these principles must be unconditionally binding . . . or, conversely, they see the truth that among different nations moral valuations are necessarily different and then infer from this that no morality is at all binding. Both procedures are equally childish.[17]   ✕

Clearly, Nietzsche does not consider his own views to be relativistic in this way. A favorite formulation of Nietzsche's moral views, "Nietzsche holds that no morality is at all binding because moral evaluations are culturally variable," must be discarded. Even those who claim that this is what Nietzsche's views amount to must at least give him the benefit of the doubt at the outset, for this simplistic formula is not what he understood his ethical views to be asserting.

Beginning with relativism, however, is always a mistake, since 'relativism as such' is in some respects more vague than 'perspectivism as such'. At least 'perspective' readily uses the metaphor of vision, just as 'point of view' does. We might therefore start instead with a *person's perspective*,

---

17. Nietzsche, *The Gay Science* 345.

and proceed from these fundamental intuitions: the metaphoric associations we discover in the simple case are undoubtedly a covert presence in all discussions of perspectivism.

In everyday parlance an individual's 'perspective' is probably understood as that person's idiosyncratic take on the world and his place in it. Historical events, random chance, his language, his upbringing, and his culture will have a particular significance for that person, a significance that no other person can wholly share. Subjectivity is implied: even though the events that shape a person are objective, shared events and ideas, the way in which these events and ideas are internally experienced and constituted is ultimately private. A passage from George Eliot's *Middlemarch* expresses this sense of 'perspective':

> Your pier-glass or extensive surface of polished steel made to be rubbed by a housemaid, will be minutely and multitudinously scratched in all directions; but place now against it a lighted candle as a centre of illumination, and lo! the scratches will seem to arrange themselves in a fine series of concentric circles round that little sun. It is demonstrable that the scratches are going everywhere impartially, and it is only your candle which produces the flattering illusion of a concentric arrangement, its light falling with an exclusive optical selection. These things are a parable. The scratches are events and the candle is the egoism of any person now absent.[18]

Members of a community will have many events and experiences in common; however, these objective events, 'scratches', will always receive private, individual limning that gives those events a personal significance and order. The complicated network of a person's beliefs and desires about her friends, relatives, and co-workers, her vocations and avocations, the community and culture she participates in, normally provides her with a sense of coherence: surely, this is the 'everyday' understanding of what a perspective is. Each person has his or her own sense of the shape of things, yet these multiple sensibilities are made possible by a particular environment and historical climate that reinforces and encourages those behaviors. Eliot's pier-glass analogy implies that a still more objective account is available in order to understand what each of her characters is 'really' seeing. This 'intuitive' meaning of what makes up a perspective is thus fairly pejorative: any pronouncements 'from my perspective' will be heard as personal, tendentious, and sorely in need of an objective account.

---

18. George Eliot, *Middlemarch* (Oxford: Clarendon Press, 1986), chap. 27.

Nietzsche's perspectivism is about something more interesting than mere subjective experience. In fact, here is where the intuitive visual metaphor fails. A person's subjective sense of herself and her world, Nietzsche claims, is only the *experience* of those environmental and historical elements that actually do constitute her perspective. For example, if I sit in a chair and see a birdcage in front of me, my perspective is not just my view of the birdcage, but also *the location of the chair* that allows me to see the birdcage. In his most famous remarks about perspectivism in *The Gay Science* 374, Nietzsche disallows the distinction between the subjectivity of a perspective and the more objective accounts that surround it:

> How far the perspective character of existence extends, or indeed whether existence has any other character than this; whether existence without 'sense', does not become 'nonsense'; whether, on the other hand, all existence is not essentially actively engaged in interpretation — that cannot be decided by the most industrious and most scrupulously conscientious analysis and self-examination of the intellect; for in the course of this analysis the human intellect cannot avoid seeing itself in its own perspectives, and only in these.

According to this passage, we may have (and undoubtedly we do have) different interpretations of our experience, with different goals in mind and various hidden assumptions at work. Some interpretations will undoubtedly be more objective and probative than others, but no account will be 'nonperspectival'. Alexander Nehamas, in his helpful remarks on perspectivism, insists that an account claiming to be impartial and objective will not on those grounds qualify as a 'nonperspectival' account.

> Nietzsche's perspectivism consists, in the main, of an attack against the idea that any particular human method for understanding the world can be assigned a privileged position, that any specific scheme can be considered as an accurate representation of the world, or of some part of it, as it really is.[19]

We will avoid the problematic final clause, "as it really is," and focus for the moment on the following characteristics of Nietzsche's view: first, every sort of human knowledge is an interpretation. No method of understand-

---

19. Alexander Nehamas, "Immanent and Transcendent Perspectivism in Nietzsche," *Nietzsche-Studien* 12 (1983): 473.

ing the world is complete, and no particular method can be 'completed' by somehow adding up all available views, because the integrity, purpose, and point of each investigation would thus be lost. Finally, the conclusions of any particular method for securing knowledge are always open to revision, either from within its own investigative principles, or by being supplanted by another method from without.[20]

We will concern ourselves with only one aspect of perspectivism, namely, the perspectival insistence on selectiveness.[21] Any method for establishing knowledge must select the elements that will be included, and this selection will be determined by the principles that make that method or discipline the one that it is. This version of perspectivism is notably humble. It does not, for example, assert that 'everything is interpretation', although that notion is certainly implied. The dictum 'everything is an interpretation', insofar as it can be made sense of, does tell us that no particular account of the world is the final, or foundational, or singular, or real, account of the world. On the other hand, to say that every account is partial and selective in its view is to say much the same thing without implying that some complete 'text' lies beneath the manifold interpretations provided. With these emendations in mind, we may reconsider the illustration from *Middlemarch*: the demonstration that the scratches on the mirror are 'really' going everywhere is no less selective in its account than the seeming halo of scratches created by the candle's light is. Each perspective on the glass simply gives us a different selection of elements, and for different (yet equally valid) reasons. Of course, this characterization makes the co-presence of perspectives far too easy. Some perspectives will inevitably 'compete' with others. A scientific account and a sociological account can be thought of as 'different perspectives', or different kinds of accounts, while, for example, Christianity and Buddhism seem to be truly competing, that is, trying to give the same sort of account.

The troubling vagueness of perspectival talk becomes apparent when we try to explain what distinguishes competing from noncompeting perspectives. There are two importantly dissimilar notions of 'difference'

---

20. Chapter 2 of Nehamas's *Nietzsche: Life as Literature* is a lengthy discussion of this point.

21. Nehamas remarks, "To engage in any activity and, in particular, in any inquiry, one must necessarily be selective. One must bring some things into the foreground and distance others into the background . . . others must be completely ignored. We do not and cannot begin with all the data" (*Nietzsche: Life as Literature*, p. 49). Cf. Nehamas, "Will to Knowledge, Will to Ignorance and Will to Power in *Beyond Good and Evil*"; Bernd Magnus, "The Deification of the Commonplace: *Twilight of the Idols*," in *Reading Nietzsche*, ed. K. Higgins and R. Solomon (Oxford: Oxford University Press, 1988), p. 152.

between perspectives. The first is the ordinary remark that different methods of gaining knowledge will obtain different results. The second argues that there may well be perspectives that are completely external to any possible human perspective; our human constitution bars us from adopting (or even recognizing) these alien perspectives.[22] An easy and persuasive way of emphasizing just how different one perspective can be from another is to imagine an account of the world that is unavailable to the human mind. This hyperbolic characterization is different from the usual claim that A and B are two different perspectives in the relevant sense, a claim that always implies that they are perspectives on the same thing (and not, for example, that they are representations of two different things or places). If they have nothing in common, this immensely increases the difficulty of conceiving what the shared referent could be like, or of how we could know that there were two perspectives. To propose a 'perspective' that is utterly unavailable to us creates what many readers of Nietzsche call the 'Kantian dilemma'. To say that A and B are both 'about' the world, and yet share no features, suggests the independent existence of some *non*perspectival thing that these perspectives both describe (or fail to describe, as the case may be).[23]

If we set aside this disturbing conception and focus instead on the usual sense of 'difference', we see just how feeble and perhaps uninteresting our ordinary claims about 'perspectives' truly are. The notion of an utterly discrete characterization of the world at least has a kind of conceptual clarity: A and B are absolutely different. When we return to 'ordinary difference', all of our many accounts of the world begin to look distressingly familiar. How can we identify a truly *new* perspective? In what sense can it be absolutely distinguished from every other perspective? Where does one perspective leave off and another begin? Is the edge of my visual field the limit of 'my' perspective, or can I sensibly pick out 'my' perspective at all?

A first point to emphasize is the *necessary* connectedness and fluidity of whatever it is that perspectives are. Surely this is what 'selectiveness' implies, for a perspective could only place some features in the foreground, others in the background, if it is capable of recognizing many of those very features that it does not, or cannot, incorporate. It is this sort of recognition that the more extreme claims about potential difference between perspectives want to deny. Accordingly, when those hidden fea-

---

22. This seems to be the highly problematic point of *Gay Science* 374.
23. This is the state of affairs at the end of "On Truth and Lie in a Non-Moral Sense."

tures are rearranged a new account is created, and presumably a new perspective. Perspectives are thus not sets of distinct features that can be worn and then stepped out of, like shoes. At this juncture we might think that this is a difficulty for Nietzsche's metaphor of occupying a perspectival 'corner'. A corner is a rigid meeting of two walls that can be stepped into and out of again, a perspective that can be actually occupied or merely observed from the other side of the room.

Clearly, the visual metaphor can traduce and mislead. As Maudemarie Clark reminds us:

> Knowing and seeing are two different activities . . . Nietzsche's metaphor offers us a model in terms of which to think about knowing. He uses it to suggest that we think of knowing as involving a factor analogous to perspective in the visual realm.

Clark proposes our corpus of beliefs as that factor. The 'appearance' of things, the account we give of ourselves, depends on what we currently believe, which beliefs stand unchallenged, and which beliefs are called to account. She concludes that perspectivism is an expression of Nietzsche's rejection of foundationalism: "Perspectivism amounts to the claim that we cannot and need not justify our beliefs by paring them down to a set of unquestionable beliefs all rational beings must share."[24]

Let me review what has been said thus far. First, perspectives are selective and inconclusive descriptions of what is, and 'perspectivism' is the doctrine claiming that there are infinitely many such descriptions, particular sets of beliefs: which is to say that both 'perspective' and 'perspectivism' are, in this sense, *reflective enterprises*. Both are representations, evaluations, and explicit accounts of how things are. According to this definition, the paradigm of a 'perspective' will be a discipline and the methods that compose it, such as philosophy, history, or physics. Certainly, each of these disciplines focuses on certain descriptive elements and ignores others, although one discipline may occasionally acknowledge another in passing. Thus, the physicist is engaged in giving an account in terms of mass and wavelength, the historian is concerned with documentation and the compiling of narrative, and the sociologist focuses on cultural trends and expressions of membership in distinct social groups. The answer to the question 'What happened?' for example, at the scene of a crime, will naturally elicit different answers; no one expects the

---

24. Maudemarie Clark, *Nietzsche on Truth and Philosophy* (Cambridge: Cambridge University Press, 1990), p. 130.

physicist to be concerned with the criminal's upbringing, nor the sociologist with the velocity of the bullets fired.[25]

'Perspectivism' is thus the concatenation of these disciplinary practices and methods, from the personal to the departmental level, ad infinitum. Competition between perspectives is the result of enough beliefs being held in common for serious disagreement to take place.[26] Curiously, neither this sense of 'perspective' nor 'perspectivism' captures the subjective, embodied sense of perspective with which our intuitions began. What are the private, intuitive accounts of ourselves and of the world that we ordinarily identify as 'perspectives'?

It seems that there are two kinds of 'perspective', which I will call 'articulate' and 'embodied'. An articulate perspective provides a reflective account of some sort, and does not need to concern itself with the particular brains, minds, or sets of experiences that created the body of knowledge from which the account is drawn. (Indeed, that dead metaphor works well here: a 'body' of knowledge in some sense 'replaces' actual ones.) Embodied perspectives, however, are not reflective pastimes that can be taken up or abandoned at will: each person (and perhaps groups of persons) is composed of various, to borrow Nietzsche's own image, cultural accretions formed by personal, social, and cultural developments. These accretions, unlike the readily available articulate perspectives, are hardly to be grasped, let alone altered. Recall the 'granite stratum' of *Beyond Good and Evil* 231. It is out of these deep, largely unfathomable layers of cultural experience that articulate perspectives emerge.

Embodied perspectives are largely unexamined; we dwell in them, or they in us. On the other hand, articulate perspectives are highly examined, polished, refined; inconsistencies and anomalies are rooted out, destroyed. This is simply the contrast between the reflective undertaking of marshaling and employing coherent sets of beliefs, habits, predilections, and a person's habits of life that are often inconsistent or irrational. Imagine a psychologist who advocates multiple and nonexclusive sexual relationships who is nonetheless firmly placed in a monogamous marriage. This psychologist, suddenly aware of the gulf between what she articu-

---

25. Cf. Barry Stroud's example of the master detective who reminds his assistant that the duke's murderer could not have entered the room through a particular door because it was blocked by a large table. The detective's assertion about the table does not touch on the skeptic's attack on knowledge claims about the existence of the table (or, indeed, on the existence of the external world). See his *The Significance of Philosophical Skepticism* (Oxford: Oxford University Press, 1984), pp. 102–3.

26. Cf. Clark, *Nietzsche on Truth and Philosophy*, pp. 142–43.

lates as her beliefs and her own actual habits and practices, may respond in several ways. She may eliminate the inconsistency by changing her habit (just as the daughter stops trimming the roast); she may realize that her habit is in fact fundamental to her sense of herself, and alter her espoused beliefs accordingly; or she may note the disparity between rhetoric and life and embrace the irony therein. (She may even conclude that her advice is good for many but not for herself.) Her articulations of herself necessarily dwell in the wider squalor of her embodied perspective.[27]

The novelist who creates a cast of characters far different from herself is also a revealing example. The putting on and shedding of perspectives that the novelist so readily engages in may be instructional or entertaining, but it does not mean that the novelist has in any concrete sense occupied those perspectives. Her imaginings easily outstrip her capacity to actually take up the forms of life she describes, an important point that we will return to in a moment.

Of course, the distinction here is unnecessarily keen: the division between these kinds of perspectives is not so absolute. Articulate perspectives can be seen as projections of embodied perspectives, the most available and fluid interpretations on the surface of our cultural, personal, and historical strata. Embodied perspectives exist prior to their articulations, both in an individual's life and in the life of the culture; this is what Nietzsche means when he says that "the life of emotion is older than the life of reason."

> For when the habit of some distinguishing action is inherited, the thought that lies behind it is not inherited with it (thoughts are not hereditary, only feelings): and provided it is not reproduced by education, the second generation . . . [experiences] only pleasure in the habit as such.[28]

Also:

---

27. Susan Faludi provides a wonderful example of this in *Backlash: The Undeclared War Against American Women* (New York: Crown Publishers, 1991), pp. 296–300. Michael and Margarita Levin are both outspoken antifeminists. Michael Levin, a philosophy professor at City College of New York, argues that women are 'genetically' designed for child care and household chores such as cooking, and are poor at 'masculine' pursuits such as math. When Faludi interviewed Levin at his home, she discovered not only that Levin's wife was a professor who specialized in the philosophy of math (" 'My wife is smarter than I am,' he says flatly"), but that they routinely share 'wifely' chores (at one point in the interview a son appears and wants to know if his father will teach him to cook rice).

28. Nietzsche, *Daybreak* 30.

The history of moral feelings is quite different from the history of moral concepts. The former are powerful before the action, the latter especially after the action in face of the need to pronounce upon it.[29]

When we examine a deeply rooted cultural habit, we might realize that the grounds for this piece of behavior are relevant but odious; on the other hand, we may discover that the grounds are irrelevant, or indeed relevant but archaic, but nonetheless compelling. To use a typically Nietzschean example: a person who has considered and rejected the basis for the Christian sacraments he grew up with can discover that he has a profound desire to get married. If he acts on that desire, he must reinterpret what he is proposing to do, that is, rejecting the Church's account of such a relationship while maintaining that the secular arrangement is a worthwhile undertaking. These deep attachments to vestiges of ancient rituals and behaviors are surely what Nietzsche means by 'instinct'. *NOTE*

Our 'instincts', of which Nietzsche has so much to say, are also part of our embodied perspective. In *The Genealogy of Morals* Nietzsche gives a history of the instincts:

> The situation that faced sea animals when they were compelled to become land animals or perish was the same as that which faced these semi-animals, well adapted to the wilderness . . . suddenly all their instincts were disvalued and 'suspended'. From now on they had to walk on their feet and 'bear themselves' whereas hitherto the water had carried them . . . they were reduced to thinking, inferring, reckoning . . . unfortunate creatures; they were reduced to their 'consciousness', their weakest and most fallible organ! . . . *All instincts that do not discharge themselves outwardly turn inward — this is what I call the internalization of man*: thus it was that man first ✗ developed what was later called his 'soul'.

This tale is an interesting addition to the sea trope. Here we have the pre-history of our land-loving ways. We were once sea creatures, free of the strict and calculable parameters of land. It is telling that the 'ground' to which we customarily appeal is in fact a later development. Our 'embodied' instincts have a more archaic origin in the 'joy of animal life' unencumbered by 'bad conscience'. As the demands of the social order increased, opportunities for the discharge of this instinctive energy were reduced. These impulses were thus sublimated:

---

29. Ibid., 34.

> Confined within an oppressive narrowness and regularity, man began rending, persecuting, terrifying himself . . . this languisher . . . who had to turn himself into an adventure, a torture chamber.[30]

Thus the 'land' the sea creatures were forced to adapt to was in fact their own construct; the moral ground they share is made of these thwarted instincts. Evidently, by 'putting out to sea', the free spirits are in some sense returning to a more primitive psychic condition.

A different remark about instinct appears in the *Nachlass* 440:

> Genius resides in instinct; goodness likewise. One acts perfectly only when one acts instinctively. Even from the viewpoint of morality, all conscious thinking is merely tentative, usually the reverse of morality.

Indeed, perhaps Nietzsche's most telling remark about instinct links it to 'revaluation':

> — First example of my 'revaluation of all values': a well-constituted human being, a 'happy one', *must* perform certain actions and instinctively shrink from other actions. . . . In a formula: his virtue is the consequence of this happiness. Everything good is instinct — and consequently easy, necessary, free.[31]

These 'happy acts' are the work not of ordinary, biological instinct, but of *cultural instincts*, of our deepest sensibilities, of an 'embodied perspective'. "Instinct' is perhaps a less contentious term for what the nonobjectivist view of ethical practice call 'knowledge'.

'Articulate' and 'embodied' perspectives lend a fuller sense to our initial notion of the 'active'/ 'receptive' model of the self. Articulate perspectives are composed of reflective activity, of a series of representations, evaluations, and judgments, while embodied perspectives are made up of the very 'attitudes' that are hardest to see precisely because they are constitutive, and hardly, in this sense, 'attitudes' at all. To return to our discussion of Taylor from Chapter 1: the relationship between (1) a person's deepest sensibilities and (2) the (reflective) expression that person gives to those sensibilities is an excellent model for our discussion of perspectivism. These two perspectival 'moments' in a person are not discrete, and their common struggle — on the one hand, the effort to question, analyze, and

---

30. Nietzsche, *The Genealogy of Morals*, Essay II 16; additional emphasis mine.
31. Nietzsche, "The Four Great Errors," in *Twilight of the Idols* 2.

clarify, and on the other, the ability to absorb, deflect, and guide these articulations — assists both self-preservation and self-understanding.

We must now take seriously the notion that this deep self is *not* an independent object to be measured, inspected, and quantified by a sort of 'spiritual surveyor', which is, unfortunately, what the image of 'spiritual granite' might imply. Perspectivism is, above all, the view that the investigation of everything — and particularly persons — must be perpetual. The 'perspectives' we adopt reflectively may illuminate a deeper portion of our character, "different constellations of opinion which had heretofore remained dark and unrecognizable."[32] Yet that revelation is not itself the last word: we can never announce that at last our self-examination has hit 'bedrock'. Recall Nietzsche's remark:

> Our opinions, valuations, and tables of what is good certainly belong among the most powerful levers in the involved mechanism of our actions, but that in any particular case the law of this mechanism is indemonstrable.[33]

— which is to say that even the most reliable features of a person's character cannot settle the question of what was at work in a particular piece of behavior. The notion of 'granite' is only a theoretical device. The metaphoric solidity of a person's constitution does not mean that this solidity can offer us an absolute rendering of a person. Some portions of a person may be seen as 'recalcitrant', 'atavistic', 'immovable', and so forth, but these identifications are not a final account of that person. We may become clearer about obscure parts of someone's character, but we cannot provide an algorithm for their actions on the basis of character, because even a clearer view of essential characteristics is not an end of the matter: "the law of this mechanism is indemonstrable." The configuration of any action is irreducibly unique. This perspectival conclusion disallows a final rendering of an individual, despite any apparent solidity of their behavior: the interpretive task is infinite.

Having separated out two senses of perspective, it might be useful to return to our previous example of a person's shifting attitude toward marriage. As always, Nietzsche has several mordant — if hardly univocal — remarks on the subject (although the nasty remarks undoubtedly outweigh the approving ones). We may now see his objectivist attitude toward the concepts at work in marriage as part of his *reflective* project,

---

32. Nietzsche, *Assorted Opinions and Maxims* 58.
33. Nietzsche, *The Gay Science* 335.

which is the work of an articulate perspective; however, sometimes he indicates that there may be a possibility of having a reconstituted form of marriage. "When entering a marriage, one should ask the question: do you think you will be able to have good conversations with this woman right into old age? Everything else in marriage is transitory." Furthermore, "The best friend will probably get the best mate, for a good marriage is based on a talent for friendship."[34] The potential for the 'revaluation of the value of marriage' is left open; these remarks indicate that a reconstituted form of marriage will rest primarily on embodied values, rather than reflective ones. This idea is expressed less happily in *Twilight of the Idols*:

> Witness modern marriage. It is obvious that all sense has gone out of modern marriage: which is, however, no objection to marriage but to modernity. . . . With the increasing indulgence of love matches one has simply eliminated the foundation of marriage. . . . One never establishes an institution on the basis of an idiosyncrasy . . . one establishes it on the basis of sexual drive, the drive to own property (wife and child considered as property), the drive to dominate which continually organizes the smallest type of domain.[35]

If we follow Nietzsche's usual approach, the way to 'revalue' marriage is not to try to revive the institution and its structure of rules, prohibitions, and so forth, but to discover the *instincts* that continue to urge people to marry. Presumably we will discover a number of hidden practices, some based on prestige, others on caretaking, or reproduction, or companionship, and so forth. Rather than being governed from without, as the earlier institution was, modern marriage will be a matter of expressing a number of cultural instincts, and thus a number of ways of life. In this respect Williams's description of the 'nonobjectivist' resembles Nietzsche: the nonobjectivist is not persuaded that the failure of ethical practices indicates that the practices themselves were not a kind of knowledge. In fact, Nietzsche seems to believe that once the corrosive of reflection has done its purgative work, the 'instincts' that were buried beneath the clutter of moral self-deception will re-emerge. We may now return to the mysterious finale of *Daybreak* 103:

> It goes without saying that I do not deny—unless I am a fool—that many actions called immoral ought to be avoided and resisted, or that

---

34. Nietzsche, *Human, All Too Human* 406 and 378.
35. Nietzsche, "Expeditions of an Untimely Man," in *Twilight of the Idols* 39.

ONLY MEANINGFUL CHANGE IS EVOLUTIONARY *

many called moral ought to be done and encouraged — but I think the one should be encouraged and the other avoided *for other reasons than hitherto.* We have to learn to *think differently* — in order at last, perhaps very late on, to attain even more: to *feel differently.*

Once reflection has dismantled the moral structure, we will be able to think differently about our behavior, and we will be disinclined to make universal moral claims and prescriptions. But that will not be the end of the matter. Nietzsche asserts that we will perhaps be able to feel differently about our practices. Instead of relying on, for example, a piece of moral dogma to bolster a particular local practice, we will instead keep up our practice on other grounds, because we find the practice beautiful (by our lights), or because it gives us joy. This does not mean that the practice is therefore immune to reflective onslaughts; on the other hand, that practice need not respond to such attacks on reflective grounds, since its 'sense' is not itself a reflective assertion.

III

We investigated perspectivism with the hope that the doctrine of perspectivism would somehow provide us with an antidote to reflection. Having separated out two senses in which we 'have' (that is, adopt, dwell in) a perspective, we may now consider the manner in which these two dimensions of perspectivism might serve to limit reflection. In general, perspectivism provides a kind of theoretical balance by reminding us that no discipline is capable of providing an exhaustive account of the world and its contents, and that no interpretation is in principle unrevisable. In particular, Nietzsche considers reflection to be 'limited' by perspectivism in two ways. The first is not really a limitation as such, but a practical consideration. Our reflective powers cannot give us the kind of knowledge that can replace traditional judgments. The disrupted members of our hypertraditional society cannot somehow 'reflect their way' back into some other set of practices, because traditional practices are characteristically inherited, not instituted by rational fiat.[36] Once a culture has be-

---

36. Likewise, Williams remarks, "There is no route back from reflectiveness . . . no way in which we can consciously take ourselves back from it" (*Ethics and the Limits of Philosophy*, p. 163). Cf. Kierkegaard in *The Present Age*: "He (the individual) finds himself in the vast prison formed by . . . reflection . . . he can only escape from this imprison-

come skeptical about the grounds for their view of sexual practices and concomitant restrictions, it will be difficult to maintain the traditional institutions in the face of this skepticism.

Any philosopher, progressive thinker or revolutionary who does not take this limitation of reflection seriously enough is, in Nietzsche's estimation, actively — albeit naively — leveling his own culture. Again, this 'limitation' is not a limit, but a warning: reflection cannot reproduce the traditional beliefs it dismantles. This is part of the reason why Nietzsche so viciously attacks David Strauss in the first of his *Untimely Meditations*. Nietzsche feels that Strauss, the paradigmatic skeptic and atheist, has become cheerful in his old age about precisely the wrong things. The work for which Strauss is most famous, *The Life of Jesus Critically Examined*, is a good example of how reflection can dismantle traditional views. In it Strauss claims that the figure of Jesus is a mythical one, composed of biblical myth and the mythologized accounts given by his contemporaries. By Nietzsche's lights (at least by the time of *The Gay Science*) the philosophical reaction to this dismantling of Christianity should be one of abject horror. Recall the Madman who announces the death of God:

> 'All of us are his murderers. But how did we do this? How could we drink up the sea? Who gave us the sponge to wipe away the entire horizon?' . . . It has been related further on the same day the madman forced his way into several churches and there struck up his *requiem aeternam deo*. Led out and called to account, he is said . . . to have replied. . . . 'What after all are these churches now if they are not the tombs and sepulchers of God?'[37]

Compare the hysteria of the Madman to the following remark from Strauss's final work, *The Old Faith and the New*:

> As if meditation were only possible in a church, edification only to be found in a sermon! Why hold fast by an antiquated, exhausted, form, at a time and in a state of culture, when there flow so many other and

---

ment through the inwardness of religion" (trans. Alexander Dru [New York: Harper and Row, 1962], p. 48).

37. Nietzsche, *The Gay Science* 125. I will not attribute these more mature insights to the Nietzsche of 1872. Nietzsche's interest in the first of his *Untimely Meditations* is, for the most part, the advent of what he calls 'German philistinism'. Of course, Nietzsche's investigation of why it is that his culture refuses to own up to the implications of rising scientism and positivism is undoubtedly connected to his later announcement of the death of God at the unwitting hands of popular culture.

more abundant sources of intellectual stimulus and moral invigoration? *After all, it is nothing but habit.* It is so difficult to think of the place as empty where something used to stand.[38]

Strauss's complacent atheism completely misses the point: if the spiritual center has truly disappeared from the life of nineteenth-century Germany, what will take its place? The "other more abundant sources of intellectual stimulus" will not necessarily provide the sort of stability and focus that the Church provided. In fact, Nietzsche warns, these pursuits may serve as a diversion from deeper and more painful cultural issues.

> We all know how our age is typified by its pursuit of science . . . almost no one asks himself what the consequences of such an involvement with the sciences could be for culture. . . . For the nature of scientific man . . . contains a real paradox: he behaves like the proudest idler of fortune, as though existence were not a dreadful and questionable thing but a firm possession guaranteed to last forever. . . . The heir of but a few hours, he is ringed about with frightful abysses, and every step he takes ought to make him ask: Whither? Whence? To what end? But his soul is warmed with the task of counting the stamens of a flower . . . he . . . is absorbed in this work.[39]

Nietzsche asserts that Strauss is merely a reconstituted member of the faithful. "He announces with admirable frankness that he is no longer a Christian, but he does not wish to disturb anyone's peace of mind."[40] In pursuing traditionally thorny philosophical and artistic issues, "the sole proviso was that everything must remain as it was before, that nothing should at any price undermine the 'rational' and the 'real'."[41] Nietzsche's conclusion? "Strauss has not yet even learned that no idea can ever make

---

38. David Strauss, *The Old Faith and the New: A Confession*, trans. Mathilde Blind (London: Asher and Co., 1874; 3d ed.), 2:119; emphasis mine. The presence of both Strauss and Eliot in this chapter is an irony worth noting. In 1841 Eliot translated Strauss's *The Life of Jesus Examined*. Of Eliot, Nietzsche remarked, "They have got rid of the Christian God, and now they feel obliged all the more firmly to cling to Christian morality: that is English consistency, let us not blame it on little bluestockings à la Eliot" ("Expeditions of an Untimely Man," in *Twilight of the Idols* 5). Hollingdale makes the editorial observation that Nietzsche had probably not even read Eliot.

39. Nietzsche, "David Strauss, The Confessor and The Writer," in *Untimely Meditations*, trans. R. J. Hollingdale (Cambridge: Cambridge University Press, 1983), p. 35.

40. Nietzsche, "David Strauss," p. 29.

41. Ibid., p. 11.

men better or more moral, and that preaching morals is as easy as finding grounds for them is difficult."[42]

Certainly, reflection poses problems that traditional beliefs cannot answer, but which nonetheless demand answering; however, this characterization underdescribes the reflective process. After the difficult questions about our religious, ethical, social, and aesthetic beliefs have been asked, a decision about how we will live must still be made. One response is Straussian complacency (which amounts to a reflective denial): we have our technology, our cathedrals and works of art; why not simply live in them and enjoy them? According to Nietzsche, this is an insidious self-deception, a denial that our moral and social grounds have shifted. Is there an alternative response? *Daybreak* 61 offers a suggestion:

> These serious, upright, deeply sensitive people who are still Christians from the very heart: they owe it to themselves to try for once the experiment of living for some length of time without Christianity, they owe it to their faith in this way for once to 'sojourn in the wilderness' — if only to win for themselves the right to a voice on the question whether Christianity is necessary. For the present they cleave to their native soil . . . *Christianity is, after all, only a litle corner!* No, your evidence will be of no weight . . . until you have wandered far, far away from it. Only if you are driven back, not by *homesickness* but by *judgment* on the basis of a rigorous comparison, will your homecoming possess any significance! — The men of the future will one day deal in this way with all evaluations of the past; *one has voluntarily to live through them once again, and likewise their antithesis* — if one is at last to possess the right to pass them through the sieve. (Emphasis mine)

This passage suggests two familiar remarks that Nietzsche later makes in *The Gay Science*. First, recall his claim in 374 that "we cannot look around our own corner: it is a hopeless curiosity that wants to know what other kinds of intellects and perspectives there might be." We cannot look around our own corner because the corner in question is our *embodied* perspective, our cultural inheritance, the 'genetic' make-up of our instincts and emotions. Nietzsche always insists that these inherited features are, for the most part, immutable. To think that we can overcome this inheritance through an enlightened and cheerful goodwill is to commit the same error that Strauss does. On the other hand, we *are* creatures of reason and

---

42. Ibid., p. 30.

imagination; even though the life of reason is younger, and the 'educable loam' above the inherited granite strata is quite thin, we may still continue to create more interpretations of ourselves. We may produce *articulate* perspectives, which will ultimately be assimilated by our cultural heritage.

Second, the notion of 'homesickness' is very important. *Gay Science* 124 makes such an observation: "Woe, when you feel homesick for the land as if it offered more freedom — and there is no longer any 'land'." The seafarers suffering from homesickness have in fact destroyed the 'land' themselves, and yet now they yearn for it. Nietzsche reminds us that simply longing for the recrudescence of absolute moral grounds is not enough to warrant an attempted return; such a turning back will be both self-deceived and fruitless. Homesickness will not be enough, but 'judgment' will be. This judgment is not a *reflective* consideration, but an acceptance of whatever 'instincts' remain after the practices in question have been 'passed through the sieve'. And something does remain: we may have (to borrow from Williams) 'confidence' in these practices. This notion of 'confidence' is quite Nietzschean. Although we did not choose the traditions and practices that socialized us, it will be the case that after reflection some of these notions will be untenable, while others will still appeal. The concepts that continue to move us are the ones in which we can have confidence.[43] These behaviors will not seem as stable as the ones of our cultural past, but Nietzsche urges us to take joy in them anyway:

> In the midst of the ocean of becoming we awake on an island no bigger than a boat, we adventurers . . . for how soon may a wind not blow us away or a wave not sweep across the little island, so that nothing more is left of us! But here . . . we find other birds of passage and hear of others still who have been here before, and thus we live in a precarious minute of knowing and divining.[44]

This ability to endorse particular inherited instincts rests on what we might call perspectivism's second limitation of reflection. Embodied perspectivism is a reminder that we overestimate our reflective powers if we think that they can completely subvert our habits, attachments, and rituals. Embodied perspectivism stands as an actual, material, and emotional limit. Even if we faithfully follow the reflective thread there is no guarantee that its conclusions will be instituted. Nietzsche indicates that we may

---

43. Williams, *Ethics and the Limits of Philosophy*, p. 170.
44. Nietzsche, *Daybreak* 314.

return to some of our old practices, although they have been permanently
altered by reflective considerations.

IV

So we are set forth into the sea, with 'Oedipus eyes' and 'Odysseus ears':

> To confront man henceforth with man in the way in which, hardened
> by the discipline of science, man today confronts the rest of nature,
> with dauntless Oedipus eyes and stopped-up Odysseus ears, deaf to
> the siren songs of old metaphysical bird-catchers who have all too long
> been piping to him 'you are more! you are higher! you are of a different
> origin!' — that may be a strange and extravagant task, but it is a task —
> who would deny that? Or to ask the question differently: 'why knowl-
> edge at all?' Everyone will ask us that.[45]

This passage makes an intriguing error. After all, Odysseus's ears were not
stopped with wax — only his sailors' ears were plugged to prevent them
from hearing both the sirens' song as well as Odysseus's pleas to change
the ship's course.[46] In remarking on this puzzle, Karsten Harries observes
that Nietzsche is actually urging us to be about the business of metaphysical deafness.

> Like Odysseus, Nietzsche would seal the ears of his fellow sailors to
> this siren song, as he would seal his own ears were he only able to do
> so. We should not forget that, when Nietzsche speaks of standing
> before the riddle that is man . . . he is stating a task.[47]

---

45. Nietzsche, *Beyond Good and Evil* 230.
46. Kafka also makes this mistake in one of his shorter stories, "The Silence of the Sirens."

> To protect himself from the Sirens Ulysses stopped his own ears with wax and had
> himself bound to the mast of his ship. Naturally any and every traveler before him
> could have done the same . . . but it was known to all the world that such things
> were of no help whatever. . . . But Ulysses did not think of that . . . he trusted to
> his handful of wax. . . . Now the Sirens have a still more fatal weapon than their
> song, namely their silence.

Franz Kafka, *The Complete Stories*, trans. Willa and Edwin Muir, ed. Nahum N. Glatzer (New
York: Shocken Books, 1971), pp. 430–31.
47. Harries, "The Philosopher at Sea," p. 32.

Certainly a task is presented, but is it simply the renunciation of our traditional philosophical desires? Surely not, for the lives of both Oedipus and Odysseus suggest a denial of something in full and intimate knowledge of what is being rejected. Both men know what it is they can no longer act upon. Oedipus's blindness does not obliterate his memory of Thebes and his relation to the city; it was his mental acuity, his 'keen eyesight', in effect, that led to his blindness. Oedipus knows all too well what it is that he can no longer see and preside over. Likewise, Odysseus must hear the sirens' song; to stop up his ears would be to miss the lesson altogether. He needs to hear what it is he cannot have, and yet know that he cannot have it. Hence, in order to fulfill Nietzsche's philosophical directive, the prolepsis 'deafness'; Odysseus's ears must be, impossibly, open and closed at the same time, which is effectively what lashing him to the mast amounts to.

In *The Birth of Tragedy* Nietzsche calls this the ability to

> see . . . and at the same time . . . get beyond that seeing. . . . Those who have never had the experience of having to see at the same time that they also longed to transcend all seeing will scarcely be able to imagine how definitely and clearly these two processes coexist and are felt at the same time. . . . But all truly aesthetic spectators will confirm that among the peculiar effects of tragedy this coexistence is the most remarkable.[48]

The 'metaphysical solace' provided by tragedy is only created in the alembic of acute vision: the audience member must be willing to see the horror of individual existence in order to see beyond it, to take joy in being vital and alive.[49] Nietzsche goes on to remark:

> We now understand what it means to see tragedy and at the same time to long to get beyond all seeing: referring to the artistically employed dissonances, we should have to characterize the corresponding state by saying that we desire to hear and at the same time long to get beyond all hearing.

---

48. Nietzsche, *The Birth of Tragedy*, section 24.

49. Here Nietzsche criticizes Aristotle for giving a superficial account of the emotions engendered by tragedy: the emotion of the tragedy is not a purgative but a surge of delight in the suffering of others.

The sea odyssey Nietzsche proposes is one that requires a complicated self-awareness. The task is not simply to join in the destruction of the ground of our traditional claims, nor is it the useless pursuit of what we have lost; rather, we must see what we have done, understand the profundity of these changes, and yet affirm what remains.

We can get an even clearer sense of *Beyond Good and Evil* 230 by considering the sequence of ideas from 229 to the momentous 231. Section 229 begins with the remark that all higher culture is based on cruelty; the paradigm of this cruelty is the tragedy. (Evidently anticipating his description of Odysseus, Nietzsche names this tragic affect the 'great Circe cruelty'.)

Working against the development of higher culture (that is, resisting or providing respite from such development) is the 'fundamental will of the spirit', the will to appearance. In order to acquire knowledge, the knower must fight this fundamental desire; he must be 'cruel' to himself by denying himself the comforts of simplicity, completion, reduction. The knower must problematize what seems self-evident. Section 24 is a useful elaboration of this:

> What strange simplification and falsification mankind live in! One can never cease to marvel once one has acquired eyes for this marvel! How we have made everything around us bright and easy and free and simple! How we have known how to bestow on our senses a passport to everything superficial, on our thoughts a divine desire for wanton gambolling and false conclusions! How we have understood from the beginning how to retain our ignorance so as to enjoy an almost inconceivable freedom, frivolity, impetuosity, bravery, cheerfulness of life, so as to enjoy life! And only *on this now firm and granite base of ignorance* has knowledge hitherto been able to rise up, the will to knowledge on the basis of a far more powerful will, the will to non-knowledge, to the uncertain, to the untrue! (Emphasis mine)[50]

Section 230 provides a similar commentary on this 'will to non-knowledge'. The 'man of knowledge' is thus not simply repudiating error and simplification, he is owning up to it: he understands the debt his knowledge claims owe to an 'artificial, fabricated, falsified world'; he can 'look and go beyond that look', 'hear and go beyond that hearing'.

---

50. See also *Beyond Good and Evil*, sections 40 and 59.

V

A person's embodied perspective, and indeed the perspectival accretions that make up a culture, answer the reflective charge precisely by not answering it: when a person leaves his critique of a particular practice and returns to the actual exigencies of his life, then we have evidence for what has survived his critical scrutiny and what has not. Whatever remains does so not on reflective grounds, but on the grounds of that individual's (embodied) judgment, namely, "I will live, and identify myself, in this manner." Providing any further considerations is to enter the reflective arena once again. Reflection just stops, not because it has a reason to stop, for that is a reflective concern, but because the individual examining his life becomes concerned with other matters, such as local notions of what constitutes comfort, or well-being, or what is, here and now, a challenge to him.[51] Nietzsche considers reflection an invaluable occupation but not the only valuable one, and clearly not the *arche* of every occupation's importance. Certainly, from the point of view of our embodied concerns, the power of reflection is remarkably feeble. As in the verse from Mallarmé that begins this chapter, the siren song of the sea draws our minds and imaginations but may not, ultimately, refashion our lives. Our ability to propose revolution often exceeds our ability to foment it. Nietzsche's infamous declaration of war against our moral tradition is also, at times, an admission of the limits of such an attack.

Having considered the conflict between reflection and embedded instinct, we can now name the individuals actually engaged in this Nietzschean struggle. Nietzsche's free spirits seem to be paradigmatic 'hyperreflectors', and their chief delight is waging conceptual war on the values currently at work in the culture. "The 'real world' — an idea no longer of any use, not even a duty . . . let us abolish it! (Broad daylight . . . return of cheerfulness . . . all free spirits run riot)."[52] The 'Übermensch', however, must 'overcome' this gleeful destruction by effacing the opposition between the free spirits and the values that they attack (values, we might add, out of which the free spirits have themselves emerged). This evolution in consciousness as borne out by these characters is the subject of Chapter 3.

51. Cf. Wittgenstein's observation: "As if giving grounds did not come to an end sometime. But the end is not an ungrounded proposition, it is an ungrounded way of acting" (Wittgenstein, *On Certainty*, section 110).
52. Nietzsche, "How the Real World at Last Became a Myth," in *Twilight of the Idols*.

3

Psychology

'noon' and 'shadow'

Doctor, have you ever seen nature double? When the sun's at
noon and it's as if the whole world was going up in flames?
That's when a terrible voice spoke to me.
— Büchner, *Woyzeck*, scene 8

Any account of Nietzsche's
metaphors of the self must eventually confront his most elusive persona,
the Übermensch. This 'character' is never explicitly introduced in Nietzsche's writings, although I argue that glimpses of 'it' are indeed available in
Thus Spake Zarathustra. In attempting to describe the Übermensch, I
shall begin by reviewing the 'cast of characters' that Nietzsche presents us
with in the first chapter of *Zarathustra*, namely, the camel, the lion, and
the child. This familiar passage describes a metamorphosis from one form
of existence to the next; in it I shall look for the antecedents of what is
usually regarded as the final Nietzschean incarnation of the individual.

Zarathustra's discourses begin with this famous announcement:

> I name you three metamorphoses of the spirit: how the spirit shall
> become a camel, and the camel a lion, and the lion at last a child.
>
> There are many heavy things for the spirit, for the strong, weight-
> bearing spirit in which dwell respect and awe: its strength longs for the
> heavy, the heaviest.
>
> What is heavy? thus asks the weight-bearing spirit, thus it kneels
> down like the camel and wants to be well laden.
>
> What is the heaviest thing, you heroes? so asks the weight-bearing
> spirit, that I may take it upon me and rejoice in my strength.[1]

---

1. Nietzsche, "Of the Three Metamorphoses," in *Zarathustra*, Part 1.

The camel is evidently an emblem of what Nietzsche calls the 'higher man', the person of culture, the scholar wholly aware of his custodial burden.[2] When this 'camel-spirit' reflects on this way of life, however, the reflective question gets raised: "Why should I bear the weight of my cultural heritage? Why is it necessary to transmit these practices and values, and not others?" In other words, what is the value of these values? In raising these skeptical questions about his cultural inheritance, the camel is transformed into the lion.

> But in the loneliest desert the second metamorphosis occurs: the spirit here becomes a lion; it wants to capture freedom and be lord in its own desert. It seeks here its ultimate lord: it will be an enemy to him and to its ultimate God, it will struggle for victory with the great dragon. What is the great dragon which the spirit no longer wants to call lord and God? The great dragon is called 'Thou shalt'. But the spirit of the lion says 'I will!'. . . .
>
> My brothers, why is the lion needed in the spirit? Why does the beast of burden, that renounces and is reverent, not suffice?
>
> To create new values — even the lion is incapable of that: but to create itself freedom for new creation — that the might of the lion can do.
>
> To create freedom for itself and a sacred No even to duty: the lion is needed for that, my brothers.[3]

The lion — the 'freier Geist', the 'free spirit' — is a familiar and consistent character in Nietzsche's writings. This persona often appears in earlier works (in fact, *Human, All Too Human* is subtitled "A Book for Free Spirits"). Consider the following description of the free spirit:

> A man is called a free spirit if he thinks otherwise than would be expected, based on his origin, environment, class and position, or based on prevailing contemporary views. He is the exception: bound spirits are the rule; the latter reproach him that his free principles have their origin either in a need to be noticed, or else may even lead one to

---

2. Bernd Magnus gives an entertaining account of this person: "For the scholar whose camel-spirit would bear much, for example, there are the obvious tools to acquire — languages (the more the better), literatures (the more the better), histories (the more the better), methodologies (the more the better). And the scholar who would bear much knows the weight of his burden; the iron discipline, the pleasures deferred, the genteel poverty. He knows all too well the musty odor of books within dank library walls while children laugh and celebrate life on sun-drenched walls outside" (Bernd Magnus, *Nietzsche's Existential Imperative* [Bloomington: Indiana University Press, 1978], p. 35).

3. Nietzsche, "Of the Three Metamorphoses," in *Zarathustra*, Part 1.

suspect him of free actions, that is, actions that are irreconcilable with bound morality. . . .

Incidentally, *it is not part of the nature of the free spirit that his views are more correct, but rather that he has released himself from tradition*, be it successfully or unsuccessfully.[4]

Hence, the lion's sacred "no". The free spirit is in the business of raising reflective issues, of creating a skeptical climate. In generating this skeptical liberation, however, the lion also creates a dilemma. Even though its task is to assert 'I will', the lion is not itself in a position to create new values — not because there are no new practices to endorse or new beliefs to promulgate but because all of these will themselves be susceptible to the skeptical questions: why this value? What are the grounds for this claim?

The character of the lion thus suggests the following general question of nihilism: how will an individual live in this negative, destructive condition? In "The Three Metamorphoses" the image of the child is proposed as an answer:

But tell me, my brothers, what can the child do that even the lion cannot? Why must the preying lion still become a child?

The child is innocence and forgetfulness, a new beginning, a sport, a self-propelling wheel, a first motion, a sacred Yes.

Yes, a sacred yes is needed, my brothers, for the sport of creation. The spirit now wills its own will, the spirit sundered from the world now wins its own world.

The child is, of course, emblematic of the Übermensch, and the Übermensch has the capacity to 'affirm' that which the Lion can only 'negate'. Unfortunately, this answer does not tell us anything. What sort of affirmation? In what way does this affirmation prevent the recrudescence of the skeptical question?

Whereas Nietzsche is prolix on the matter of bound spirits — the 'Higher Men' — as well as the free spirits fomenting revolution, he does not tell us much about the Übermensch. This reticence is itself of some interest. First, the term 'Übermensch' makes a late appearance in Nietzsche's work. The only work chiefly concerned with the Übermensch is *Thus Spake Zarathustra* (although a description of the eidetic moment in which the

---

4. Nietzsche, *Human, All Too Human* 225; emphasis mine.

notion emerged, "6000 feet above man and time," is, of course, later offered in *Ecce Homo*).

The standard characterizations of the Übermensch in the critical literature are fairly vague. Some commentators think that descriptions of the Übermensch are in principle misguided, because the Übermensch is necessarily incomprehensible to us as we are currently constituted (namely, all-too-humanly). Those writers who do give us some sort of account usually offer us an 'Overman' who is simply a more perfected version of the free spirit and the higher man. This Übermensch is a hybrid—a free spirit *not* suffering from a restless inability to stop overthrowing norms, joined with a 'higher man' who is not burdened by the Spirit of Gravity, one who joyfully celebrates his cultural inheritance.[5] Of course, it is Nietzsche himself who makes this last reading possible, not through his description of the Übermensch (since he never provides us with one) but through the teachings that Zarathustra offers his listeners and the instructions he gives them. This, from the "Prologue," is pardigmatic of Zarathustran rhetoric:

> I teach you the Overman. Man is something that should be overcome. What have you done to overcome him?
>
> All creatures hitherto have created something beyond themselves and do you want to be the ebb of this great tide, and return to the animals rather than overcome man?
>
> What is the ape to men? A laughing-stock or a painful embarrassment. And just so shall man be to Overman: a laughing-stock or a painful embarrassment . . .
>
> The Overman is the meaning of the earth. Let your will say: the Overman shall be the meaning of the earth! . . .
>
> Man is a rope, fastened between animal and Overman—a rope over an abyss . . .
>
> What is great in man is that he is a bridge and not a goal; what can be loved in man is that he is a going-across and a down-going.

Commentators generally conclude that the Übermensch is a creature (for indeed, Zarathustra announces in "The Vision and the Riddle" that the

---

5. Magnus's description of the Übermensch is representative of this popular 'hybrid' approach: "Like the child of the three metamorphoses, the integration of intelligence, strength of character and will, autonomy, passion, taste, and prowess have become natural in the Übermensch. The form he has given his life now is his life . . . the Übermensch is . . . not burdened by derivation from the lives of others. He lives his life in authentic self-possession" [!] (*Nietzsche's Existential Imperative*, p. 38).

Übermensch is no longer human)[6] that has perfected what Nietzsche takes to be the highest human types. This creature is a goal, a being that does not yet exist, but a being for whose existence humankind should now strive.[7] Even at this provisional interpretive stage, however, we must be suspicious. If Nietzsche truly intends humanity to pursue a univocal goal of any kind then he is committed, it seems, to endorsing something like a universal or transcendent ideal, a proposal clearly anathema to Nietzsche's other, more baldly stated (anti-)aims. Certainly, this 'ideal' is emphatically denied by Zarathustra himself in "The Spirit of Gravity":

> All my progress has been an attempting and a questioning — and truly, one has to learn how to answer such questioning! That however — is to my taste: not good taste, not bad taste, but *my* taste, which I no longer conceal and of which I am no longer ashamed.
>
> 'This — is now my way: where is yours?' Thus I answered those who asked me 'the way'. For *the* way — does not exist!

We might say, instead, that the Übermensch is not an ideal for everyone, but for only those exceptional individuals who are his rightful genealogical predecessors; the Übermensch will still be an ideal, even if his followers are limited in this way. Nietzsche, however, did not intend this character to figure as an idealized goal, at least not in some straightforwardly normative sense. For example, these remarks in *Ecce Homo*:

> The word 'Overman' to designate a type that has turned out supremely well, in antithesis to 'modern' men, to 'good' men, to Christians and other nihilists — a word which, in the mouth of a Zarathustra, the destroyer of morality, becomes a very thoughtful word — has almost everywhere been understood with perfect innocence in the sense of those values whose antithesis makes its appearance in the figure of a Zarathustra: that is to say as an 'idealistic' type of species of higher species of man, half 'saint', half 'genius'.[8]

---

6. Although this remark can hardly be taken literally in light of the following passage from *The Anti-Christ* 3: "The problem I raise here is not what ought to succeed mankind in the sequence of the species (— the human being is an end —): but what type of human being one ought to breed, ought to will, as more valuable, more worthy of life." Cf. Nietzsche, *Human, All Too Human* 247).

7. The stock ending of *Thus Spake Zarathustra* commentaries is vague but cheerful (in an aporetic way), usually alluding to the hopeful, elusive metaphor of the child who 'now wins his own world'.

8. Nietzsche, "Why I Write Such Excellent Books," in *Ecce Homo* 1, trans. R. J. Hollingdale (New York: Penguin Books, 1979).

Evidently, and contrary to the usual Zarathustran exhortations, we are not meant to regard the Übermensch as a regulative ideal. I suggest that the image of the Übermensch as some not yet existent but perfect 'creature-goal' is itself misleading, despite the passages that offer us such an image. By focusing on Zarathustra's teachings and experiences we may conclude, oddly enough, that there is not a discrete character called the Über-mensch, and that in fact the name 'Übermensch' designates a particular dimension of the experience of the free spirits. Whether or not a way of life lies beyond these two dimensions of experience is something considered at the end of this chapter.

I shall proceed by giving a close reading of the metaphors that Nietzsche uses in *Thus Spake Zarathustra*, beginning with the sequence of meta-phors in "The Vision and the Riddle." This passage is traditionally read as an important formulation of the Eternal Return, yet this reading overshad-ows its remarkable implications for the nature and constitution of the Übermensch. The Eternal Return has its own abundance of complications, and rather than atttempting to unpack simultaneously two sets of issues I shall set it aside for the moment. Provisionally, we may con-sider the Übermensch and the Eternal Return of the Same as two parts of a single directive of affirmation;[9] the intimacy of these two notions will require consideration elsewhere. This controversial and difficult moment in the text will also provide us with a preliminary sketch of the two central metaphors Nietzsche uses to describe the free spirit's psychology: noon and shadow.

II

"The Vision and the Riddle" begins with Zarathustra onboard a ship, telling a group of sailors how he had carried a dwarf, called the Spirit of Gravity,

---

9. A normative understanding of the Eternal Return is not universally acknowledged. In this, as in other respects, the notion leaves in its wake a great deal of controversy. Scholars are inclined to make strange assertions on its behalf, such as the astonishing remarks of John Andrew Bernstein in *Nietzsche's Moral Philosophy* (Cranbury: Associated University Presses, 1987): "Here I assume, along with the majority of scholars, that Nietzsche meant by [the Eternal Return] exactly what he said: that all things that happen now have happened before and will happen again an infinite number of times in the future" (p. 55). In support of this claim Bernstein cites "Of the Vision and the Riddle," in *Zarathustra*, Part 3, section 2 — which of course makes it unclear why this is *Nietzsche's* claim, rather than Zarathus-tra's; moreoever, it is not even self-evidently what Zarathustra is claiming.

up a mountain path. At section 2 of the passage the dwarf jumps down, and their conversation continues:

> 'Behold this gateway, dwarf!' I went on: 'it has two aspects. Two paths come together here: no one has ever reached their end. This long lane behind us: it goes on for an eternity. And that long lane ahead of us — that goes on for another eternity.
>
> They are in opposition to one another, these paths, they abut on one another: and it is here at this gateway that they come together. The name of the gateway is written above it: 'Moment'. . . .
>
> 'Behold this Moment!' I went on. 'From this gateway Moment a long eternal lane runs back: an eternity lies behind us.
>
> 'Must not all things that can run have already run along this lane? Must not all things that can happen have already happened, been done, run past?'

This statement is the beginning of one of the important formulations of the Eternal Return. But the vision continues; suddenly Zarathustra is in a second scene:

> Where had the dwarf now gone? And the gateway? And the spider? And all the whispering? Had I been dreaming? . . . But there a man was lying! And there! . . . And, truly, I had never seen the like of what I then saw. I saw a young shepherd writhing, choking, convulsed, his face distorted; and a heavy, black snake was hanging out of his mouth . . . the snake had crawled into his throat — and there it had bitten itself fast.
>
> My hands tugged and tugged at the snake — in vain! They could not tug the snake out of the shepherd's throat. Then a voice cried from me: 'Bite! Bite! Its head off! Bite!' Thus a voice cried from me, my horror, my hate, my disgust. . . .
>
> You who take pleasure in riddles! Solve for me the riddle that I saw, interpret to me the vision of the most solitary man! . . .
>
> Who is the shepherd into whose mouth the snake thus crawled: Who is the man into whose throat all that is heaviest, blackest will thus crawl?
>
> The shepherd, however, bit as my cry advised him; he bit with a good bite! He spat far away the snake's head and sprang up.
>
> No longer a shepherd, no longer a man — a *transformed being, surrounded with light, laughing!* Never yet on earth had any man laughed as he laughed!

> O my brothers, I heard a laughter that was no human laughter — and now a thirst consumes me, a longing that is never stilled. (Additional emphasis mine)

Heidegger's treatment of this passage is a useful place to begin. Heidegger considers the images of the gateway and the shepherd to be necessarily connected. He claims that the biting off of the snake's head is the 'moment' in which the shepherd grasps (rather gruesomely) the meaning of the Eternal Return, and it is this understanding that transforms him. The snake is thus the nihilistic reality of the 'formal sameness' of all things — which is roughly what Heidegger thinks the Eternal Return is — and *the moment* is the instant when its implications are accepted.

It seems clear that these images are meant to be read together, for the less philosophical reason that there is an obvious isomorphism. The Augenblick (literally, 'the blink of an eye') — the Moment — is a gateway from which two paths stretch, one designated the 'past', the other the 'future'. Likewise, the shepherd's mouth is also a gateway from which two opposed entities stretch. Of course, later on Zarathustra will identify the snake as his 'disgust for man', which is certainly a *historical*, temporal designation: a disgust with the sum of human history replete with pettiness, malfeasance, and stupidity. Heidegger remarks, "Only by way of nihilism and the moment is the eternal recurrence of the same to be thought. Yet in such thinking the thinker as such slips into the ring of eternal recurrence, indeed in such a way as to help achieve the ring, decide it."[10] And what is this thought of Eternal Recurrence? Heidegger claims that it is the realization that all one can ever do is move forward into local, particular, and contingent cultural possibilities that are already provided. The two sides of this 'conquering thought' turn out to be depressing indeed. Regardless of whether we see our values and the lives we fashion from them as meaningful or meaningless, it is all alike. What is 'all alike' is that all of our activities are finally (metaphysically) the same; that is, they are all the exercise of the will to power, of the will overcoming itself. What perpetually occurs is the positing of value in order that it be overcome. The person who understands this — who accepts it and wills it — is (according to Heidegger) the Übermensch.[11]

---

10. Heidegger, *Nietzsche*, vol. 2, p. 182.
11. For example, this characteristic passage:

> The essence of the Over-man consists in stepping out 'over' the man of the past. The latter needs and seeks ideals and idealizations 'above' himself. Overman, on the

Heidegger's interpretation focuses on the Eternal Return as the enabling thought: the shepherd with the snake in his mouth is taken to be a help in understanding what it is that Zarathustra tells the dwarf. On such a reading, the Übermensch just is the being who wills the Eternal Return in this way, and so we focus on what it means to think this thought.

The reverse procedure, however, is also illuminating. We may view the gateway Moment as an illustration, a foretaste, of what the biting off of the snake's head is meant to signify. And indeed, an amazing thing happens when the shepherd bites: we see an Übermensch come into being. This moment of creation is even more interesting when we consider who that shepherd is. The shepherd is Zarathustra, and he himself tells us this in "The Convalescent," where he remarks to his animals:

> 'Oh you buffoons and barrel-organs!' answered Zarathustra and smiled again, 'how well you know what had to be fulfilled in seven days: and how that monster crept into my throat and choked me! But I bit its head off and spat it away. And you — have already made a hurdy-gurdy song of it? I, however, lie here now, still weary from this biting and spitting away, still sick with my own redemption.'

The Übermensch of the Augenblick may thus be tentatively identified as a transmogrified Zarathustra, who is "no longer a man, a transformed being, surrounded by light, laughing."[12]

If one can become an Übermensch in 'the blink of an eye', in some sort of transcendent Moment, perhaps we should briefly turn our attention to the phenomenology of these Moments; indeed, several such Moments appear in *Zarathustra*. First, consider a passage from Part 4 called "At Noontide":

> About the hour of noon, however, when the sun stood exactly over Zarathustra's head, he passed by an old gnarled and crooked tree which was embraced around by the abundant love of a vine and hidden from itself. . . . Then he felt a desire to relieve a little thirst

---

contrary, no longer needs the 'above' and 'beyond', because he alone wills man himself, and not just in some particular aspect, but as the master of absolute administration of power with the fully developed power resources of the earth.

It is inherent in the essence of this man that any particular substantive aim, any determination of such kind, is always a nonessential and purely incidental means . . . he recognizes the essential indeterminateness of absolute power.

12. Nietzsche, "Of the Vision and the Riddle," in *Zarathustra*, Part 3.

and to pluck himself a grape; but when he had already extended his arm to do so, he felt an even greater desire to do something else: that is, to lay down at the hour of perfect noon and sleep. . . . In falling asleep, however, Zarathustra spoke thus to his heart: 'Soft! Soft! Has the world not just become perfect? What has happened to me? . . . Just see — soft! old noontide sleeps, it moves its mouth: has it not just drunk . . . an ancient brown drop of golden happiness, of golden wine? Something glides across it, its happiness laughs. Thus — does a god laugh. . . . Precisely the least thing, the gentlest, lightest, the rustling of a lizard, a breath, *a moment, a twinkling of the eye — little* makes up the quality of the *best* happiness. Soft! What has happened to me? Listen! Has time flown away? Do I not fall? Have I not fallen — listen! into the well of eternity?[13]

The above passage contains some powerful expressions — in particular, 'perfection' and 'eternity', both terms of completion and affirmation. This is a moment of transformation in which the world becomes perfect, when Zarathustra's disgust is momentarily healed. He calls this experience 'falling into the well of eternity' and likens it to a god's laughter, a remark reminiscent of the laughing god at the end of "The Vision and the Riddle." We might therefore conclude that 'the Moment' is the moment of self-acceptance, the moment when Zarathustra can say 'yes' to himself and find himself annealed, completed, quenched, and finished: his yearning for humanity's distant goal is satisfied. Certainly, Zarathustra tells us that self-love is a demanding art: "And, truly, to learn to love oneself is no commandment for today or for tomorrow. Rather is this art the finest, subtlest, ultimate and most patient of all."[14] This embracing of oneself may in fact be only the precursor to the transformative noontide moment. "And he who declares the Ego healthy and holy and selfishness glorious — truly, he, a prophet, declares too what he knows: 'Behold, it comes, it is near, the great noontide!' "[15] We might, on the basis of this evidence, postulate the Übermensch as a being created by, and dwelling in the Augenblick, the Moment, a moment in which all differences vanish, in which the highest form is realized. I shall set this aside as a possible formulation and return to it later in this chapter.

Of course, the Augenblick is only one approach to the Übermensch. The other form of what we might call 'Overman-discourse' is the more familiar,

---

13. Nietzsche, "At Noontide," in *Zarathustra*, Part 4; emphasis mine.
14. Nietzsche, "Of the Spirit of Gravity," in *Zarathustra*, Part 4.
15. Nietzsche, "Of the Three Evil Things," in *Zarathustra*, Part 3.

namely, that the Übermensch is a goal toward which human beings are meant to strive. By overcoming one's most cherished beliefs (such as the need to affirm a coherent and moral universe) a person will start to make his way across the bridge from 'man' to 'Overman'; the latter expression is a typical formulation. Many such remarks are made in the course of the *Zarathustra*:

> And although you are high and of a higher type, much in you is crooked and malformed. There is no smith in the world who could hammer you straight for me. You are only bridges: may higher men than you step across upon you! You are steps: so do not be angry with him who climbs over you into his height!
>
> From your seed there may one day grow for me a genuine son and perfect heir: but that is far ahead. You yourselves are not those to whom my heritage and name belong. . . .
>
> This guest-gift do I beg of your love, that you speak to me of my children. In them I am rich . . . what would I not give, to possess one thing: these children, this living garden, these trees of life of my will and of my highest hope![16]

Here Zarathustra advocates not a sublime instant of self-acceptance but utter rejection of one's self. Zarathustra denies the way in which he and these higher men are currently constituted in favor of those who will come later, his 'children'. He remarks, "The Overman lies close to my heart, he is my paramount and sole concern — and not man: not the nearest, not the poorest, not the most suffering, not the best."[17] Indeed, it is these children who provide Zarathustra with his ultimate purpose.

> Thus I am in the midst of my work . . . for the sake of his children Zarathustra must perfect himself. For one loves from the very heart only one's child and one's work; and where there is great love of oneself, then it is a sign of pregnancy: thus I have found.[18]

Zarathustra thus describes a task for each person: the creation of a personal, idiosyncratic goal, a standard for each person alone in virtue of which that person can be said to be 'pregnant'. This perfected self is not

---

16. Nietzsche, "The Greeting," in *Zarathustra*, Part 4.

17. Nietzsche, "Of the Higher Man," in *Zarathustra*, Part 4.

18. Nietzsche, "Of Involuntary Bliss." I will have more to say about Zarathustra's 'pregnancies' and 'children' in Chapter 4.

identical with the person in question but only 'related', as a child is to a parent. The person may be identified as having given birth to that perfected self, but he will not be that self. Indeed, an early reference to 'Overmen' in *The Gay Science* describes just such a relationship:

> For an individual to posit his own ideal. . . . The wonderful art and gift of creating gods. . . . It was here that the luxury of individuals was first permitted. . . . The invention of gods, heroes, and overmen (Übermenschen) of all kinds . . . was the inestimable preliminary exercise for the justification of the egoism and sovereignty of the individual.[19]

But even if we remove these 'gods' from an 'Overworld', as we are obviously meant to do, and relocate them as each individual's personal creation and ideal, there is an equally obvious gap between the image the person creates and that person. It is this lack that makes the person suffer, since he or she has not yet embodied that ideal. This is the pain that Zarathustra is willing to endure for the sake of his 'children'.

Self-overcoming entails precisely this sort of suffering. A free spirit struggles to overcome his or her attachments, habits, irrational beliefs, pieces of faith, and so forth, in order to be free of them, and this divestment of self is usually quite painful. In the passage "Of Self-Overcoming" Zarathustra remarks:

> And life itself told me this secret: 'Behold,' it said, 'I am that which must overcome itself again and again.
>
> To be sure, you call it will to procreate or impulse towards a goal, towards the higher . . . but all this is one and one secret.
>
> I would rather perish than renounce this one thing; and truly, where there is perishing and the falling of leaves, behold, there life sacrifices itself—for the sake of power!
>
> That I have to be struggle and becoming and goal and conflict of goals: ah, he who divines my will surely divines along what crooked paths it must go!
>
> *'Whatever I create and however much I love it—soon I have to oppose it and my love: thus will my will have it.'*[20]

---

19. Nietzsche, *The Gay Science* 143.
20. Nietzsche, "Of Self-Overcoming," in *Zarathustra*, Part 2.

Here is yet another reminder that the Übermensch cannot be a 'goal' in the ordinary sense, for that goal would also have to be overcome. Thus far, our characterization of the Übermensch indicates that this being is different from that which must overcome itself, different in some as yet unspecified sense.

The Übermensch is a 'whole', completed being, and in this essential respect seems 'different' from the process of self-overcoming. Certainly, the 'laughing god' of "The Vision and the Riddle" does not need or desire anything. Of course, the free spirit who would overcome himself is necessarily *not* whole, because he lacks the qualities of his ideal self. The process of self-overcoming always involves two aspects: the free spirit as currently constituted and that which the free spirit opposes, either the values of his culture, or his own beliefs, habits, and practices. And, of course, the free spirit overcomes these values in virtue of yet another set of evaluations, which in turn must be overcome.

The image of a person and his shadow is an important emblem of the free spirit's psychic division: his 'self and other self'. The shadow's presence is a useful opportunity for self-reflection: it allows that person to examine and consider a shifting variety of auto-images. A shadow also suggests mutability, an image of the self that changes shape depending on the light in which it is viewed. Zarathustra's Shadow apparently suffers the division and conflict of being a free spirit.

> 'But I have fled to you and followed you longest, O Zarathustra, and although I have hidden myself from you, yet I was your best shadow: where you have sat there I sat too. . . .
>
> 'I have broken up with you whatever my heart revered. I have overthrown boundary stones and statues, I have pursued the most dangerous desires — truly, I once went beyond every crime. . . .
>
> 'Nothing is true, everything is permitted': thus I told myself. I plunged into the coldest water, with head and heart. . . .
>
> 'What is left to me? A heart weary and insolent; a restless will; infirm wings; a broken backbone. . . .
>
> 'This seeking for my home: O Zarathustra, do you know this seeking was my affliction, and it is consuming me. . . .
>
> Thus spoke the shadow, and Zarathustra's face lengthened at his words. 'You are my shadow!' he said at length, sorrowfully. 'Your danger is no small one, you free spirit and wanderer!'[21]

---

21. Nietzsche, "The Shadow," in *Zarathustra*, Part 4. The result of this state of siege is exhaustion; cf. *The Gay Science* 309.

The Shadow's (and, by implication, Zarathustra's) self-overcomings have left him bereft. It is interesting, however, that this passage immediately precedes one previously discussed, 'At Noontide', which describes the Augenblick, the Moment in which Zarathustra 'falls into the well of eternity'; and, of course, at the hour of perfect noon all shadows are effaced. It is no doubt important, and something to be ultimately considered, that the Shadow's account of his desperate pursuits is followed by one of completion and perfection in the Moment.

Who, indeed, is the Shadow? This question is charmingly posed in the peripatetic framework to Part 3 of *Human, All Too Human*, "The Wanderer and His Shadow." The Wanderer speculates that his Shadow is his vanity, but the Shadow points out that while a person's vanity is never silent, his Shadow is only now beginning to speak. The Shadow is in fact the Wanderer's power to doubt, to call his view of himself into question. This is why the Shadow, rather than the Wanderer, issues the invitation to speak. The Shadow claims that he is cast by the sunlight of knowledge, and is its necessary adjunct. Thus the Shadow is not — and this is crucial — the hackneyed 'darkness of ignorance', but the 'darkness' of an unanswered question, the anticipation of that which is to be known. Moreover, the kind of 'light' will determine the quality of 'shadow'. If the 'light' is that of vulgar endoxa then the Shadow becomes less of a skeptic and more of a philosopher. "He (the philosopher) avoids glare, and for this reason he avoids his own time and the 'light' of his day. In this he is like a shadow: the more the sun goes down, the larger he grows."[22] The Wanderer's shadow, however, becomes weaker as the sun goes down. The light of knowledge, unlike the 'light' of current fashion, is allied to the capacity to question, to doubt. The Shadow remarks that he is always sorry to disappear because he is "greedy for knowledge." He asserts, paradoxically, that less darkness would cling to humankind if shadows were omnipresent; the skeptical penumbra ultimately deepens and clarifies our accounts of the world (a somewhat facile view, perhaps, given the problems of skepticism considered in Chapter 2).

What the Shadow wants is a kind of completion. As he says to Zarathustra: "Where is — my home? I ask and seek and have sought for it, I have not found it." Zarathustra cautions him that he is in danger of making a home for himself in some sort of comfortable dogmatism. "Take care that you are not at last captured by a narrow belief, a hard, stern illusion! For hence-

---

22. Nietzsche, *The Genealogy of Morals*, Essay III, section 8.

forth everything that is narrow and firm will entice and tempt you."[23]
Zarathustra sends the Shadow to his cave for a rest cure, and then leaves
him for the bliss of Noontide: "I will run alone, so that it may grow bright
around me." The darkness of a cave as well as the brightness of 'perfect noon' both 'complete' the shadow by eliminating it; the contrast of
light and dark — that is, the contrast of claim and question, the division of
self and questions about that self, is destroyed.

The narcosis of night and the blaze of noon both destroy shadows, and
perhaps this is why Zarathustra cries out in "The Drunken Song": "Midnight is also noonday." His world has, as he says, become 'perfect', that is,
perfectly unshadowed. The Wanderer and his Shadow, however, suggest
another kind of completion, one that "loves shadow as much as light." The
Wanderer exclaims, "For there to be beauty of face, clarity of speech,
benevolence and firmness of character, shadow is as needful as light. They
are not opponents: they stand, rather, lovingly hand in hand, and when
light disappears, shadow slips away from it." This affirmation of the division that characterizes the free spirit is followed by a warning: the Wanderer reminds himself that the time with the Shadow is brief. Certainly, the
free-spirited assault can only be fitfully carried out; skepticism too has its
limits.[24]

The exchange between the Wanderer and his Shadow ends with a
curious remark. The Shadow insists that even though he follows close
behind, he is no slave to the Wanderer. "When man shuns the light,
we shun man: our freedom extends that far." The capacity to wonder,
to question, depends on the Wanderer's commitment to the search for
knowledge. Furthermore, the Shadow suggests that he might agree to
becoming the Wanderer's slave if the reward were a 'perfect knowledge of
man'. The Wanderer, however, also makes a plea for a kind of freedom.
Rather than be enslaved by his doubting side — surely what a Nietzschean
version of a 'perfect knowledge of man' would entail — he wants their
relations to remain 'playful'; that is, characterized by the usual round of
reflective postures, the momentary respite of 'unshadowed', undoubted
claims.

And with that, the reflective hour is over. The Shadow, like Diogenes,

---

23. Nietzsche, "The Shadow," in *Zarathustra*, Part 4.

24. Cf. this remark from the *Nachlass* (cited by Marianne Cowan in her introduction to
Philosophy in the Tragic Age of the Greeks [New York: Gateway Editions, 1962], p. 18): "No
one converses with me beside myself and my voice reaches me as the voice of one dying.
With thee, beloved voice, with thee, the last remembered breath of all human happiness, let
me discourse, even if it is for another hour."

asks the Wanderer to step out of the light. The allusion to the famous
anecdote about Alexander is intriguing. Alexander, who famously admired
the Cynic Diogenes, visits him in his clay tub and asks if there is anything
that he wants. "Get out of my light," he says.[25] The Shadow's demand is
different—he wants less light; he wants to be blotted out by shade. The
Shadow goes further than Diogenes. He not only calls worldly values and
acquisitions into question, he retreats from them, and from the attack on
them, altogether.

When the Wanderer's shadow-side disappears he is no longer a full-
fledged free spirit. The free spirit is necessarily a divided soul, staking
claims that he is ultimately compelled to call into question. Nevertheless,
the struggle of self and shadow-self is exhausting, and the free spirit wants
to attain some kind of wholeness. Both the Shadow and the Wanderer
express a desire for union, completion, psychic soundness. In the eponymous first section of Part 3 of *Thus Spake Zarathustra*, the Wanderer
(Zarathustra) remarks, "It is returning, at last coming home to me—my
own Self and those parts of it that have long been abroad and scattered
among all things and accidents. . . . Only now do you tread your path of
greatness! Summit and abyss—they are now united in one!" Despite this
hopeful declamation, however, Zarathustra is still not at peace with himself. He admits that his greatest journey of self-discovery has yet to begin,
and that even greater solitude and sorrow await him.

III

Now that we have a clearer sense of the free spirit as both Wanderer and
Shadow, we can return to the question of who, or what, an Übermensch is.
Recall that the Übermensch is above all some sort of ideal, a 'goal' the free
spirit restlessly moves toward. Recall also that two dimensions in the

---

25. This story has many versions, including Arrian's *Campaigns of Alexander* 7.2, and
Plutarch's *Alexander* 14. Of this meeting Peter Green remarks:

> This shows shrewd percipience. Both men shared (and surely recognized in each
> other) the same quality of stubborn and alienated intransigence. But whereas Dio-
> genes had withdrawn from the world, Alexander was bent on subjugating it: they
> represent the active and passive forms of an identical phenomenon. It is not sur
> prising, in the circumstances, that their encounter should have been so abrasive.
> *Alexander of Macedon* (Berkeley and Los Angeles: University of California Press,
> 1991), p. 123.

genesis of the Übermensch have been revealed: first, the constant self-overcoming, the shadowed wandering, in which an image of an Übermensch is conceived, an image on the basis of which the free spirit becomes the 'bridge' to the Übermensch, and second, the moments in which an individual is actually able to embrace him- or herself and accept all that he or she is. This distinction is a disturbing one because the Übermensch is usually characterized as a being that brings these two aspects together. He is supposed endlessly to re-invent himself *and* to overcome himself in a wholly affirming manner. As I have shown, however, these attitudes, in their very constitution, are opposed to one another.

How does Heidegger treat this problem? Heidegger claims that the Übermensch is the person who has properly embraced the Eternal Return, which he understands as 'the essential sameness of all activity': whatever a person does is just more will to power, the will always willing the overcoming of itself. Any particular level of power obtained must always be overcome, in perpetuity. The Übermensch, in understanding this (metaphysical) sameness of activity, erects values only in order to overcome them. The 'moment of affirmation' of the Übermensch is therefore just this recognition that everything is essentially will to power, and that the only point of adopting a value is to overcome it.

Heidegger's account conflates self-overcoming, in which a will is not satisfied with itself, with the moment of self-affirmation, which wills that everything should remain eternally the same. In order to decide whether or not Heidegger's interpretation is plausible, we must think about the *content* of the moment in which the Eternal Return is grasped. Is this moment an *experience* that a person has "in the blink of an eye" (*ein Augen-Blick*), or is it a *thought* that one has in a blinding, ecstatic moment? The first case of course includes the second, but the question is whether it is the content of the thought, or merely having it, that contains its value. Does the value of the Augenblick lie in a *thought* that one carries away from that moment?

Nietzsche does not adopt this sort of consequentialist approach to the Augenblick. In his descriptions of other, similar ecstatic moments it is the moment so experienced that is valued, not what a person can take away from it. So the final remarks of *Beyond Good and Evil*:

> Alas, and yet what are you, my written and painted thoughts! Is it not long ago that you were still so many-colored, young and malicious . . . and now? You have already taken off your novelty and some of you, I fear, are on the point of becoming truths . . . no one will divine from these how you looked in your morning, you sudden

sparks and wonders of my solitude, you my old beloved — wicked thoughts![26]

It is not merely that there is a difference between the instant of inspiration and the words Nietzsche records in memory of it. An importance is attached to these moments of divination — of artistic vision — themselves, an importance that the articulation of such moments lacks. They are not, nor can they be, that which is described.

Heidegger, however, focuses on the content of the Augenblick's thought, which for him is presumably, "Since all activity is essentially the Will to Power, in embracing myself and my life I am also willing that I do the same activity eternally: it is all alike, and I so will it." When that person 'recovers' from this moment of vision, he can return to his self-overcoming with that thought coloring his activity, and when the question of purpose is raised, that person can answer it ("It is all alike and I so will it").

On our reading, however, what characterizes the Augenblick is not any concept the moment may contain, but the phenomenon of the Augenblick itself. The Augenblick so understood is not a container for a thought but a transformation of the self. Here a crucial distinction must be drawn between the 'philosophical' reading of the Eternal Return and the 'phenomenological' reading of it. (I am ignoring a third reading — the cosmological one — not only because it is implausible, but because others have already given far more thorough and cogent arguments against it than I can provide here.)[27] The philosophical reading claims that the Eternal Return is a *thought* that one understands in a revelatory instant; after that instant, the person sees himself differently, for all eternity, by means of that thought. The phenomenological reading, on the other hand, asserts that a transformation occurs in that moment that cannot be reproduced 'in time', or in self-overcoming. Regardless of what insights a person gleans from that moment, *that moment* remains a discrete (that is, inarticulable) experience. In fact, there is little evidence that any useful insights, other than the simple memory of what the moment was like, can be carried out beyond the bounds of the Augenblick. Zarathustra, in "The Convalescent," says that he must 'recover' from it. He is "sick with his own redemption,"

---

26. Nietzsche, *Beyond Good and Evil* 296; cf. Kierkegaard's 'aesthetic' sphere, which is unarticulable. Only with the introduction of the ethical sphere is one able to articulate experience.

27. For example, Arthur Danto, *Nietzsche As Philosopher* (New York: Macmillan, 1965) and Georg Simmel, *Schopenhauer and Nietzsche*, trans. H. Loiskandle, D. Weinstein, and M. Weinstein (Amherst: University of Massachusetts Press, 1986).

which suggests that he is sick at being back in the realm of overcoming, replete with disgust and frustration.[28]

Nehamas also thinks that there is a tension in the idea of the Übermensch between the instruction 'overcome yourself' and willing the Eternal Return, but for different reasons. He claims that the central feature of the character 'the Übermensch' is his awareness of the 'fluidity', the mutability of his nature, and that this 'fluidity' explains why it is that constant self-overcoming is emphatically associated with the Übermensch.[29] I have already considered some of these remarks from the "Prologue" of *Zarathustra*, which do indeed endorse the dissolution of the stable self in favor of a being that constantly seeks to re-invent itself. Rather than viewing constant self-overcoming as opposed to self-affirmation, however, Nehamas claims that self-overcoming is the *vehicle* of self-affirmation. The focal thought of the Übermensch, as Nehamas describes him, is the continuous desire that everything that happens be exactly as it is. In other words, the Eternal Return is a psychological test in which a person might pose the following questions to herself: "If the history of the world were played out again, would I want to change my behavior? Would I want to alter my affiliations, desires, choices?" If a person is no more, but no less, than her 'history' (a confederacy of beliefs, events, anecdotes, and so forth, that is no doubt always undergoing some form of reconstruction), then only the complete acceptance of that history will amount to a complete acceptance of herself. The person who can accept herself as composed of both the unavoidable stupidities and accidents as well as the successes that figure in a life has attained the 'highest possible form of affirmation'.

Now, in imagining a being whose life is only a continual willing that everything be as it is, there are two difficulties. First, our power to take charge of the future, and thus 'create ourselves' in such a form that we would gladly eternally will it, is limited. Second, it is difficult to explain how it is that we can go about accepting parts of our past that we find humiliating or worthless; coming to terms with a piece of behavior is not

---

28. Cf. Nietzsche's remarks in *Ecce Homo* when he discusses the insights he has had '6000 feet above man and time', insights that presumably found some expression in *Zarathustra*.

29. "The fluidity of character in turn explains why the eternal recurrence can function as the 'highest formula of affirmation that is at all attainable' (EH III, on Z, 1). The discussion in the section 'On Redemption' (Z, II, 20) suggests that a life can be justified only if it comes to be accepted in its entirety. The mark of this is the desire to repeat this life, and so everything in the world as well, in all eternity. This means that we should want nothing in that life and the world to be in any way different" (Nehamas, *Nietzsche: Life as Literature*, p. 159).

the same as affirming that behavior.[30] Nehamas's solution to the conflict between the process of self-overcoming and self-affirmation is to exclude the transfiguring Moment. The joy experienced by the Übermensch is simply the pleasure he takes in fashioning and refashioning the narrative that he is. This approach, however, does not answer the questions that we have encountered: how do we reconcile affirmation and overcoming as they are characterized in *Zarathustra*? How can the moment in which one wills that everything be eternally the same be *integrated* with a life principled on dissatisfaction? To do or be in one of these dimensions is precisely not to do or be in the other.

This tension is one way of understanding what Zarathustra calls his "twofold will." Even though Zarathustra claims that he rejects the all-too-human in favor of the advent of the Übermensch, he also has ties to the realm of self-overcoming:

> It is not the height, it is the abyss that is terrible!
> The abyss where the glance plunges downward and the hand grasps upward. There the heart grows giddy through its twofold will.
> Ah, friends, have you, too, divined my heart's twofold will? . . .
> My will clings to mankind, I bind myself to mankind with fetters, because I am drawn up to the Overman: for my other will wants to draw me up to the Overman.[31]

Even at the end of the book these two dimensions are still in opposition, although admittedly the opposition is a curious one. The imagery of "The Drunken Song" straightforwardly takes up the images of "The Vision and the Riddle" as well as that of "At Noontide." At the beginning of the passage Zarathustra announces that midnight has arrived, and that 'time has fled': "Do I not sink into deep wells?" As in "The Vision and the Riddle," there is a howling dog beneath the moon. In section 6 of "The Drunken Song" the bell of midnight is, oddly enough, "ripe like golden autumn and afternoon" from which "an odor is secretly welling up, a scent and odor of

---

30. Nehamas characterizes 'willing that everything be the same' as an ever-present interpretive challenge for the Übermensch; that is, there must be a kind of perpetual narrative activity that constructs a coherent and meaningful life out of what Zarathustra calls 'dreadful riddle and accident'. This narrative must grapple with a person's intentional actions as well as the coincidences and misfortunes that befall her. Clearly, this process could never properly be said to have 'ended'. The 'process never ends' for many reasons, the most important of which is perspectivism: there is no transcendental place from which one can properly declare an end.

31. Nietzsche, "Of Manly Prudence," in *Zarathustra*, Part 2.

eternity . . . a brown, golden wine of ancient happiness." Finally, in section 7, Zarathustra cries, "Let me be! . . . Has my world not just become perfect?" Section 9 offers perhaps the clearest statement of the way in which affirmation is set against overcoming:

> Woe says: 'Fade! Be gone, woe!' But everything that suffers wants to live, that it may grow ripe and merry and passionate, passionate for remoter, higher, brighter things. 'I want heirs,' thus speaks everything that suffers, 'I want children, I do not want myself.'
>
> Joy, however, *does not want heirs or children*, joy wants itself, wants eternity, wants recurrence, *wants everything eternally the same.*[32]

Clearly, it is only through 'joy' that a person wants the Eternal Return. A person suffering the failures and pain of self-overcoming will naturally reject the present and focus on the future.

Section 10, however, announces that in fact these alternatives are the same. "My world has just become perfect, midnight is also noonday, pain is also joy, a curse is also a blessing, the night is also a sun — begone, or you will learn: a wise man is also a fool." Certainly, there is a perspectival point to be made here: the ecstatic vision of the Augenblick is quite different from that of self-overcoming. In the Moment it is appropriate to denounce difference, because the Moment is itself a nontemporal designation. The very medium in which difference is noted and established does not exist.[33] From the eternal vantage point of joy, the rejection issued by suffering is also embraced, yet that embrace does not reach beyond the Augenblick. It does not alter the quality of suffering for the person enduring it.

We meet again the question of the 'content' of the Augenblick. We can think of the person transported by such an ecstatic moment as having made a commitment to herself, that 'from this Augenblick forward' she will realize that in fact she has accepted her sufferings. Even though she will experience the same frustrations and denial in her projects, she will remember that they, too, have been "baptized at the fount of eternity and are beyond good and evil."[34] Even though she as sufferer will make these distinctions, she-of-the-Augenblick has permanently altered the character

---

32. Nietzsche, "The Intoxicated Song," in *Zarathustra*, Part 4; emphasis mine.

33. See, for example, Nietzsche, "The Sign," in *Zarathustra*, Part 4: "All this lasted a long time, or a short time: for, properly speaking, there is no time on earth for such things."

34. Nietzsche, "Before Sunrise," in *Zarathustra*, Part 3.

of her actions and reactions, even though this alteration is intangible in self-overcoming.

This explains how it is that 'joy is suffering', but it does not bring these phenomena any closer together.[35] In spite of these difficulties, however, it is certainly clear that Nietzsche does envisage for us some kind of redemptive *life* rather than merely a redemptive moment.

> The profound instinct for how one would have to live in order to feel oneself 'in Heaven', to feel oneself 'eternal', while in every other condition one by *no* means feels oneself 'in Heaven': this alone is the psychological reality of 'redemption'. — A new way of living, not a new belief.[36]

The problem of articulating this redemptive life remains: how is it that we can feel these contrary attitudes simultaneously? More basically: is their 'integration' in fact the task that Nietzsche sets for us?

IV

If we see Nietzsche as setting us this task of trying in our life to reconcile 'joy' and 'suffering', it is certainly a sensible interpretive strategy to set aside the Augenblick as a phenomenon to be understood separately. Yet it leaves some questions in its wake. We are left to wonder why it is that Nietzsche, from his early notebooks to his last hysterical writings, relentlessly uses this and other metaphors of illumination. What is the 'great noon', the 'perfect noon' toward which both the individual as well

---

35. Gadamer remarks on this intractable opposition in his essay "The Drama of Zarathustra." He writes:

> How can one proclaim the innocence of a child as a goal? How can the proclaimer of a new doctrine of the Overman exhort us to something that we cannot want? This is the deepest tension in the proclamation of innocence and immediacy and the eternal recurrence of the same that runs through the entire book and that is familiar to us as the old tragic inheritance of German idealism: the paradox of restored immediacy, of mediated immediacy.

Michael Allen Gillespie and Tracy Strong, eds., *Nietzsche's New Seas*, p. 222.

36. Nietzsche, *The Anti-Christ* 33. This passage reminds us, pace Heidegger, that 'redemption' is not merely a thought that one has.

as Western culture is inexorably surging? What kind of perfection and redemption does it represent?

The Augenblick of "At Noontide" represents a late stage in the development of this metaphor, which appears in most of the aphoristic works.[37] Moreover, 'noon' is only one of a broader range of references to illumination, of which the titles "Morgenröte," "Der Wanderer und sein Schatten," and "Götzen-Dämmerung" are only the most obvious instances; and, of course, light is a central metaphor for the Apollinian in "The Birth of Tragedy."[38]

The particular significance of Zarathustra's 'saying of the great noontide' lies in its suggestion of happiness, inspiration, self-effacement, and respite.[39] The 'bliss of forgetfulness' is itself present in much earlier works. In "On the Uses and Disadvantages of History for Life," Nietzsche remarks:

> Imagine the extremest possible example of a man who did not possess the power of forgetting at all and who was thus condemned to see everywhere a state of becoming: such a man would no longer believe in his own being, would no longer believe in himself . . . he would in the end hardly dare raise a finger . . . it is altogether impossible to live at all without forgetting . . . there is a degree of sleeplessness, of rumination, of the historical sense which is harmful and ultimately fatal to the living thing.[40]

This anodyne of 'sleep' is clearly present in "At Noontide." It is only after Zarathustra falls *asleep* that the world becomes 'perfect' and 'eternal'.[41]

---

37. For example, these notable passages: *Human, All Too Human* 638, *The Wanderer and His Shadow* 308, *The Gay Science*, 'Songs of Prince Vogelfrei', *Beyond Good and Evil* 296, to name a few.

38. Nietzsche occasionally draws attention to the hours of 10:00 – 12:00 P.M. as the most salubrious time of day for the philosopher. For example: "They (philosophers) ponder on how, between the tenth and twelfth stroke of the clock, the day could present a face so pure, so light-filled, so cheerful and transfigured: they seek the philosophy of the forenoon" (*Human, All Too Human* 638); "The handsomest study I ever had, on the Piazza di San Marco, given spring and the time of day between 10:00 and 12:00" (*The Genealogy of Morals*, Essay III, section 8). Of this latter description Lars Gustafsson remarks, "It almost sounds like an invitation to come and see him. What a pity he is dead!" (*Reading Nietzsche*, p. 184).

39. Nietzsche, "Of Old and New Law-Tables," in *Zarathustra*, Part 3.

40. Nietzsche, "On the Uses and Disadvantages of History for Life," in *Untimely Meditations*, section 1.

41. Here we must reject Heidegger's remarks about the 'great Noon' in "The Word of Nietzsche" (p. 102): "The great noon is the time of the brightest brightness, namely, of the

Nietzsche is equally concerned with the healthy effect of certain forms of self-dissolution. In "Schopenhauer as Educator," he writes:

> And so nature at last needs the saint, in whom the ego is completely melted away and whose life of suffering is no longer felt as his own life. . . . It is incontestable that we are all related and allied to the saint . . . there are moments and as it were bright sparks of love in whose light we cease to understand the word 'I'.[42]

Self-forgetfulness, an epiphanic moment in which differences are effaced, has an obvious embodiment for Nietzsche in the figure of Dionysus, but the hour of noon is particularly sacred to another deity, Pan. Nietzsche makes only one explicit reference to Pan[43] in *The Wanderer and His Shadow*:

> *At noon.* — He who has been granted an active and storm-filled morning of his life is overcome at the noontide of life by a strange longing for repose that can last for months or years. It grows still around him, voices recede in the distance; the sun shines down on him from high overhead. Upon a concealed woodland meadow he sees great Pan sleeping; all things of nature have fallen asleep with him, an expression of eternity on their face: — that is how it seems to him. He wants nothing, he is troubled by nothing, his heart stands still, only his eyes are alive — *it is a death with open eyes*. Then the man sees many things he never saw before, and for as far as he can see everything is

---

consciousness that unconditionally and in every respect has become conscious of itself as that knowing which consists in deliberately willing the will to power as the Being of whatever is." This description violates the stasis of sleep that Nietzsche normally insists on associating with midday. Moreover, it is a commonplace of classical pastoral poetry (Virgil's *Eclogues*, for example) that shepherds go to sleep at noon.

42. Nietzsche, "Schopenhauer as Educator," in *Untimely Meditations*, section 6.

43. Laurence Lampert dismisses "At Noontide" as being 'Emersonian', and not comparable to the great noon of Pan. He writes:

> Zarathustra reveals himself, even in his perfection and the perfection of the world, as not a simple unity of soul and spirit. . . . In his transparency to himself he remains in part female soul, tempted to remain at rest . . . and in part masculine spirit, restless to undertake his work.

This attribution of gender seems unwarranted by the passage. See *Nietzsche's Teaching* (New Haven: Yale University Press, 1986), pp. 299 and 355 n. 24.

enmeshed in a net of life and as it were buried in it. He feels happy as he gazes, but it is a heavy, heavy happiness. — Then at length the wind rises in the trees, noon has gone by, life again draws him to it, life with unseeing eyes, its train of followers sweeping along behind it: deception, forgetfulness, destruction, transience. And thus the evening rises up, more active and more storm-filled even than the morning. — To truly active men the more long enduring states of knowledge seem almost uncanny and morbid, but not unpleasant. (308; emphasis mine)

The similarities with "Mittag" in Zarathustra are striking.[44] Pan's sacred hour is noon, and to disturb him during his rest from the hunt is to risk his anger and the eponymous panic that will follow.[45] The danger of panolepsy explains why it is that Zarathustra's happiness at noon is 'sleeping', and why his respite is also 'sad'. "This golden sadness oppresses it, it makes a wry mouth." In fact, Zarathustra cautions himself that "this is the secret solemn hour when no shepherd plays his flute."[46]

Of course, the image of Pan is ambiguous. The peril of madness, of panic, is present, but this 'eternal', 'perfect' Moment is also the source of inspiration and transformation. Panolepsy is associated with divination as well as with the metamorphosis of a person from one form to another. But this inspiration is inseparable from other aspects of Pan; anyone surging toward a noontide epiphany runs the considerable risk of being lost in that rapture forever. That is why Mittag is 'a death with open eyes';[47] it is also why Zarathustra sometimes calls midday an 'Abgrund' ('non-ground').

---

44. The similarity is surely significant, although Karl Löwith believes that it should be disregarded. He writes: "Zwar ist auch die welthafte Stunde des Pan abgründig und von unheimlichen Machen bedroht, aber das Abgründige des mythischen Mittags ist nicht die Bodenlosigkeit, die Nietzsche an seines 'Lebens Mittag' fühlt" (*Nietzsches Philosophie der ewigen Wiederkehr des Gleichen*, 3d rev. ed. [Hamburg: Felix Meiner, 1978], p. 110).

45. In *The Cult of Pan in Ancient Greece*, Philippe Borgeaud remarks: "Noon is typically silent and motionless . . . Pan is the god of noise and movement; if we wake him at this hour when he should be asleep, we are in effect inviting him to fill up this silence and stillness." Borgeaud also cites this speech from Theocritus: "It is not fit, shepherd, not fit at noon for us / To play the syrinx. We fear Pan. His hunt / is over now; he's tired and rests" (Borgeaud, *The Cult of Pan in Ancient Greece*, trans. Kathleen Atlass and James Redfield [Chicago: University of Chicago Press, 1988], p. 111).

46. Nietzsche, "At Noontide."

47. Gadamer notes that in a former draft of *Zarathustra* Nietzsche considered having Zarathustra die at the end of Part 3 (*Nietzsche's New Seas*, p. 227); even though Nietzsche did not use this ending, Zarathustra still seems ambivalent (even suicidal) about the narcotic enticements of the Moment.

"When, well of eternity! serene and terrible noontide abyss! When will you drink my soul back into yourself?" Here the absolute opposition of these two experiences, the Augenblick and self-overcoming, is even further emphasized. In yearning for the great Noon we yearn for apotheosis and completion, yet we cannot also want to remain in that Moment, for that Moment (from the perspective of life) is a pause, a lacuna in the life-process. In order to want the 'great noon' we must also *not* want it, because we must also want to finish our projects in the 'evening', and conceive new ones in the 'morning'. Zarathustra leaves us hanging on this paradox at the end of Part 1:

> And this is the great noontide: it is when man stands at the middle of his course between animal and Overman and celebrates his journey to the evening as his highest hope: for it is the journey to a new morning. Then man, going under, will bless himself; for he will be going over to Overman, and the sun of his knowledge will stand at noontide.
>   All gods are dead: now we want the Overman to live — let this be our last will at the day of the great noontide!
>   Thus spoke Zarathustra.

But by the lights of Zarathustra's own reckoning, the 'day of the great noontide' is just one more epiphanic instant, simply another crest on the wave of an individual's vitality that will inevitably devolve into another form that will in turn create another Augenblick. There can be no final 'grosser Mittag'.

V

The Moment, in its favored guise as the great Noon, is thus importantly ambiguous; but so too is the process represented by that easy phrase 'self-overcoming', 'selbst-überwindung'. As we have seen earlier in this chapter, the free spirit, who struggles to overcome himself, is necessarily divided. Now we should consider the *process* of self-overcoming, which has itself been variously understood. Two models of self-overcoming need to be examined.

The first and more obvious may be termed 'aesthetic': the free spirit wants to fashion himself 'as a work of art'.[48] This is the now notorious aestheticism of Nietzsche's thinking:

> The older Greeks demanded of the poet that he should be a teacher of adults: but how embarrassed a poet would be now if this was demanded of him — he who was no good teacher of himself and *thus failed to become a fine poem*, a fair statue, but at best as it were the modest, attractive ruins of a temple . . . an object inspiring sad reflections on why the noblest and most precious must nowadays grow up straightway as a ruin without any past or future perfection.[49]

Some readers of Nietzsche emphasize the gentle, retiring, imaginative side of such behavior. Richard Rorty's account of Nietzsche, for example, amplifies this notion of 'person as poet'. He argues that the 'poet' is a supreme emblem of the self *sui generis*, composed of a new language, indeed, of utterly original metaphors.[50] Nietzsche's own conception of self-fashioning, however, is not as gentle as the image of a 'poet' suggests; as he observes in *Ecce Homo*, it is a warrior's pursuit.[51] A person so committed must attack, defend, and overthrow her own values as well as

---

48. This 'aesthetic' method is somewhat different from what Nehamas means by an 'aesthetic model' of the self (*Nietzsche: Life as Literature*, p. 165); Nehamas's aestheticism indicates a concern with form over content, with the arrangement and deployment of certain features rather than the features themselves. He contrasts this aestheticism with moral concerns: if creating a magnificent character is a person's objective, ethical deliberation seems to be permanently beside the point.

My interest in 'aestheticism' is in its 'active' quality. The 'artist', or the person coming to terms with herself, must treat that process of self-fashioning as if she were creating something entirely new, distinct, and wholly unrelated to whatever base, humiliating events preceded it. It is this attitude in Nietzsche that many commentators focus on and emphasize. On the other hand, Nietzsche's insistence that we own up to ourselves as cultural artifacts is largely neglected, and it is this contrast between the 'active creator' and the 'humble historian' that I want to suggest by my use of the terms 'aesthetic' and 'historical'.

49. Nietzsche, *Assorted Opinions and Maxims* 172.

50. See Richard Rorty, *Contingency, Irony, and Solidarity* (Cambridge: Cambridge University Press, 1989), pp. 27 - 28:

> Rather, (Nietzsche) saw self-knowledge as self-creation. The process of coming to know oneself . . . is identical with the process of inventing a new language — that is, of thinking up some new metaphors . . . To fail as a poet — and thus, for Nietzsche, to fail as a human being — is to accept somebody else's description of oneself, to execute a previously prepared program, to write, at most, elegant variations on previously written poems.

51. Nietzsche, "Why Am I So Wise?" in *Ecce Homo*, section 7.

those against which she defines herself. There can be no respite for this aggression; as soon as one ideal is embodied, it too is worthy of skepticism, of attack. "He who attains his ideal by that very fact transcends it."[52] Indeed, self-overcoming needs stable beliefs and assertions in order to have something against which it can assert itself. Zarathustra makes this observation when he describes the distant future in which the Übermensch will be realized:

> I flew, an arrow . . . out into the distant future, which no dream has yet seen . . . where all time seemed to me a blissful mockery of moments . . . where I found again my old devil and arch-enemy, the Spirit of Gravity, and all that he created: compulsion, dogma, need and consequence and purpose and will and good and evil: for must there not exist that which is danced upon, danced across: Must there not be moles and heavy dwarfs — for the sake of the nimble, the nimblest?[53]

It is interesting that even in this distant South that no one has yet seen, these dancing gods are still burdened with the Spirit of Gravity; moreover, the Spirit of Gravity (that which informs dogmatizers and believers) is evidently necessary for the dancing gods so that they may have something against which they can distinguish themselves. Nietzsche states this more baldly in the *Will to Power* 866: "[The overman] needs the opposition of the masses, of the leveled, a feeling of distance from them! He stands on them, he lives off them."[54] This parasitic relationship sounds quite different from Rorty's poet. It also hardly resembles Nietzsche's own image of the child. When a child plays, she does not usually treat the principles of the game being played as ones to be undermined, or, more properly in the metaphor, 'overcome'; rather, these rules are accepted as part of the plaything, part of the game itself. Surely 'forgetfulness' and 'a self-propelling wheel' suggest a child absorbed in play, giving no thought to whatever else surrounds her. We shall think further about this elusive child in Chapter 4.

In one respect the 'aesthetic' (namely, 'self-creating') attitude of the free spirits involves a mistake, made by its own free-spirited lights. The free

---

52. Nietzsche, *Beyond Good and Evil* 73.

53. Nietzsche, "Of Old and New Law-Tables," in *Zarathustra*, Part 3.

54. This passage from the *Nachlass* describes a man that is 'higher than the average' and that 'preserves himself under different conditions' — all good indications that what Nietzsche means by 'overman' here is simply a stronger version of free-spirited self-overcoming. These remarks are very different from Zarathustra's description of something that in every respect surpasses humankind. See also "Of the Virtue That Makes Small," in *Zarathustra*, Part 3, section 2: "Small people are necessary."

spirit deems it necessary to attack and dismantle his own values and the values of others, presumably with the aim of showing that these values are compromised or worthless. But this demonstration can only be made by bringing these values alongside another set of values *against which* they are found lacking. So, for example, a free spirit might attack religious doctrine by asserting a vigorous naturalism. Inevitably that naturalism will also find itself under attack. Thus, the way in which a free spirit deprives a particular view of grounds is by asserting others, a procedure that serves to reestablish the opposition between fiction and fact, appearance and reality, the very opposition that the free spirit wants to deny. Of course, this is noted at the end of the familiar "How the Real World Became a Myth":

> 5. The 'real world' — an idea no longer of any use, not even a duty any longer . . . let us abolish it! (Broad daylight; breakfast; return of cheerfulness and bon sens; Plato blushes for shame; all free spirits run riot).
> 6. We have abolished the real world: what world is left? the apparent world perhaps? . . . But no! With the real world we have also abolished the apparent world!
> (Mid-day; moment of the shortest shadow; end of the longest error; zenith of mankind; INCIPIT ZARATHUSTRA).[55]

The free spirits who need a set of principles to rebel against, to "stand on," recapitulate a bifurcation of the real and the unreal, the true and the untrue. Indeed, the free spirits attack the views in question as though there were a truth to be established, but any conclusion in its turn will also be 'transcended'. It is the opposition that must be denied, and it is this denial that Nietzsche deems "mid-day; moment of the shortest shadow."

---

55. Nietzsche, *Twilight of the Idols* 4. Jacques Derrida remarks:

> Thus, as the story goes, 'with the true world we have abolished the apparent one!' In such a tortured moment not only has the hierarchy of the two worlds of the sensible and the intelligible been reversed, but a new hierarchy with its new order of priorities has been affirmed. Its innovation does not consist in a renewal of the hierarchy or the substance of values, but rather in a transformation of the very value of hierarchy itself . . . What must occur then is not merely a suppression of all hierarchy, for an-archy only consolidates just as surely as the established order . . . nor is it a simple change or reversal in the terms of any given hierarchy. Rather, the *Umdrehung* must be a transformation of the hierarchical structure itself.

Spurs/Eperons, Nietzsche's Styles/Les Styles de Nietzsche, trans. Barbara Harlow (Chicago: University of Chicago Press, 1979), p. 81.

)

LESS
CLEAR

   The process of self-overcoming, however, has a second and less perspicuous model, one that makes an uneasy (and infrequent) alliance with
the sort of aggression displayed by the aesthetic attitude.[56] Sometimes the
person who struggles to overcome himself views his nature as something
to be investigated, fulfilled. He does not see the values that compose his
character as obstacles to breach, but as cultural directives to be understood. This version of self-overcoming focuses on what has already been
made of the person, through environment, upbringing, genetics, and so
forth, instead of what that person can be molded into — hence, this attitude is not "aesthetic" but "historical."[57] In this rarer mood, Nietzsche
remarks:

> The poet expresses the general higher opinions possessed by a people,
> he is their flute and mouthpiece — but, by virtue of metric and all other
> methods of art, he expresses them in such a way that the people
> receive them as something quite new and marvellous. . . . Indeed, in
> the clouds of creation the poet himself forgets whence he has acquired
> all his spiritual wisdom — from his father and mother, from teachers
> and books of all kinds, from the street and especially from the priests;
> he is deceived by his own art . . . whereas he is repeating only what
> he has learned.[58]

> Direct self-observation is not nearly sufficient for us to know ourselves;
> we require history, for the past continues to flow within us in a
> hundred waves; we ourselves are, indeed, nothing but that which at
> every moment we experience of this continued flowing.[59]

A free spirit who takes himself up in this manner will have a different
understanding of his project, of what can and should be attempted.

> And with that, forward on the path of wisdom, with a bold step and full
> of confidence! Throw off any discontent with your nature, forgive

---

56. We should note that Heidegger ascribes to the Übermensch a wholly 'aesthetic'
manner of self-overcoming. What this account neglects is examined below.

57. Ofelia Schutte seems to think that self-overcoming can be both 'active' and 'passive'
in this way. She writes, "The idea of self-overcoming is broad enough to encompass the
process of change in all of its manifestations, including the periods of relative stability"
(*Beyond Nihilism: Nietzsche Without Masks* [Chicago: University of Chicago Press, 1984],
p. 32.

58. Nietzsche, *Assorted Opinions and Maxims* 176; Certainly, this account of the poet's
activities is very different from Rorty's 'Nietzschean poet'.

59. Nietzsche, *Assorted Opinions and Maxims* 223; also 382.

yourself your own ego, for in any event you possess in yourself a ladder with a hundred rungs upon which you can climb to knowledge. . . . Do not underestimate the value of having been religious. . . . You must . . . be on familiar terms with history and with playing the cautious game with the scales 'on one hand — on the other hand'. . . . You have it in your hands to achieve the absorption of all you experience — your experiments, errors, faults, delusions, passions, your love and your hope — into your goal without remainder. *This goal is yourself to become a necessary chain of rings of culture and from this necessity to recognize the necessity inherent in the course of culture in general.*[60]

Here we see a far humbler version of the free spirit, who understands his goal as "giving ear to the voice of Nature," who considers his own nature mysterious, worthy of investigation and interpretation. The emphasis is not on the creation of some new being, but on the investigation of a being whose borders are indistinct, merging into the history of the culture that produced him.

'Self-overcoming' thus has two expressions. The *aesthetic* aspect is its 'active' dimension, a creative activity that focuses on what can be made of a person (such as a 'fine poem' or 'fair statue'). The *historical* dimension of self-overcoming, however, focuses not on what a person can become, but what a person *has* become, and so is 'receptive' in its recognition of that which the self has assimilated and emulated, of the many materials 'received' by the self. (A person thus investigating himself is, furthermore, 'receptive' in his attitude. He must be attentive and open in his self-perusal.) This attitude is different from the willfulness of the aesthetic approach, in which a person boldly asserts whatever it is that he or she must become.

The 'historical' and 'aesthetic' attitudes are evident at the end of *Zarathustra*. In "The Drunken Song" Zarathustra reassures the Higher Men that they are needed, that "all eternal joy longs for the ill-constituted," which presumably means that the culture owes its fairest products to its entire, sordid history. 'That which is overcome' is needed as well as 'that which overcomes'; the Higher Men have worth in their own, historical right.[61] Once morning arrives, however, Zarathustra returns to his former

---

60. Nietzsche, *Human, All Too Human* 292.
61. This need is different from the dancing gods 'needing' believers on which 'to stand'. This sort of need recognizes the historical necessity of all things, good and ill.

dissatisfied, bellicose, aesthetic self: he yearns for his 'children', he rejects the Higher Men, he strides forth to perfect himself.

VI

With the ambiguities of 'self-overcoming' in mind, what it means to think of the Eternal Return as "the highest formula of affirmation that can possibly be attained" can be reconsidered.[62] Willing that all things recur eternally is surely the most 'historical' of exercises. This is why Zarathustra falls into a stupor as 'the abyss speaks'. Affirming the presence of ressentiment in human history is too overwhelming a task for him: "The great disgust at man—it choked me and crept into my throat." Yet it is this acceptance that is required, an attitude Nietzsche displays in *Ecce Homo*: "How should I not be grateful to my whole life?—And so I tell myself my life."[63] The story that Nietzsche tells in *Ecce Homo* is significant in that it successfully brings together both the aesthetic and historical aspects of self-overcoming. The book is an aesthetic enterprise because it creates a Nietzsche that did not previously exist, one who is 'clever', writes wonderful books, and is a 'destiny'. He is not the Nietzsche who was forced to retire from his career at age thirty-five because of his health, who spent the remainder of his life wandering from Genoa to the Upper Engadine, who was able to create few lasting relationships, particularly with women. This latter account is also recognizably Nietzsche's history, but it is not the story he tells, and it is not the account that we are primarily inclined to give, either. When Nietzsche announces, "So I tell myself my life," he creates a new version of himself. This version, however, is not an invention or fantasy but rather a different perspective on recognizable events. In this sense the account is also historical, for in it Nietzsche must come to terms with the very moments that he might otherwise suppress.[64]

---

62. Nietzsche, "Thus Spake Zarathustra," in *Ecce Homo*.

63. This passage also notes that this sentiment arose on his forty-fourth birthday, a "perfect day, when everything has become ripe and not only the grapes are growing brown"—all evocative of the Augenblick.

64. Of this self-creation Nehamas remarks:

> One way, then, to become . . . one's own character . . . is after having written all these other books, to write Ecce Homo and even to give it the subtitle 'How One Becomes What One Is'. It is to write this self-referential book in which Nietzsche can be said with equal justice to invent or discover himself.

The ideal sort of self-overcoming requires both aesthetic and historical dimensions. Nietzsche admired Goethe precisely because he had managed to marry these different impulses, the arrogance of the artist with the humility of the historian.

> *Goethe* — not a German event but a European one: a grand attempt to overcome the eighteenth century through a return to nature, through a going-up to the naturalness of the Renaissance, a kind of self-overcoming on the part of that century. — He bore within him its strongest instincts: sentimentality, nature-idolatry. . . . He called to his aid history, the natural sciences. . . . What he aspired to was totality . . . he disciplined himself to a whole, he created himself. . . . A spirit thus emancipated stands in the midst of the universe with a joyful and trusting fatalism, in the faith that only what is separate and individual may be rejected, that in the totality everything is redeemed and affirmed — *he no longer denies*. . . . But such a faith is the highest of all possible faiths: I have baptised it with the name *Dionysus*.[65]

I began with the question: who is the Übermensch? We pursued Zarathustra's exhortations to overcome ourselves as well as his more elusive promises of respite, illumination, and perfection, and by taking both of these notions as strongly as Zarathustra (and Nietzsche) presents them, we found ourselves confronted with utter division: these notions exclude one another. Furthermore, we discovered that it is the free spirits who are described by these two psychological moments, the release of noon and the presence of the shadow. The solution to this split, which is truly not a 'solution' as such, is to retain this dualism. First, when the great Noontide is considered in its mythic aspect, we understand that this epiphany is best understood as the moment of inspiration. As Nietzsche remarks in "On the Advantages and Disadvantages of History for Life":

See *Nietzsche: Life as Literature*, p. 165.

65. Nietzsche, *Twilight of the Idols* 49. The self-effacement of the 'historical' aspect of self-overcoming is usefully contrasted with reactivity, which it is not. 'Activity'/'reactivity' is the opposition that pairs an active shaping of one's character and life with a reactive inability to do so (*ressentiment*). However, Goethe's 'Dionysian faith' is better thought of as one-half of the pair 'activity'/'receptivity'. This opposition contrasts the active shaping of one's character with a passive understanding that the features under one's control are created by external cultural forces. The former pair might be called 'noble life vs. Christian life', the latter, 'Apollinian understanding vs. Dionysian understanding'. On the contrast between Christian and Dionysian values, cf. Gilles Deleuze, *Nietzsche and Philosophy*, trans. Hugh Tomlinson (New York: Columbia University Press, 1983), pp. 13-17.

> Imagine a man seized by a vehement passion, for a woman or a great idea: how different the world has become to him! . . . It is the condition in which one is least capable of being just; narrow-minded, ungrateful to the past, blind to dangers, deaf to warnings, one is a little vortex of life in a dead sea of darkness and oblivion: and yet this condition — unhistorical, anti-historical through and through — is the womb not only of the unjust but of every just deed too; and no painter will paint his picture, no general achieve his victory, no people attain its freedom without . . . an unhistorical condition.[66]

But this vortex of inspiration, this Panic 'seizure', must be followed by a struggle to bring the vision of that Augenblick into reality. The person must return to 'history' — to the demands and responsibilities of life — and must once again confront his shadow. The desire to stay in that moment is an invitation to panolepsy, madness. It is the 'noontide abyss' that Zarathustra wishes will consume him, it is the ultimate denial of his humanity.

The Übermensch, then, is quite literally the human who is 'overcome', the person who is momentarily divested of self in a flash of insight or rapture. Clearly, that momentarily transformed person must return to the exigencies of his life, to the particular projects and concerns of which his life is made. A life in which both of these aspects properly fulfill their separate functions will, at the very least, resemble the 'redemptive life' Nietzsche describes in *The Anti-Christ* — the new way of life that is not merely a new belief but rather the 'feeling of Heaven' "while in every other condition one by no means feels oneself in Heaven." An account of this life, and its implications, is the task of Chapter 4.

---

66. Nietzsche, "On the Uses and Disadvantages of History for Life," in *Untimely Meditations*, section 1.

4

Diagnosis

the 'child' and 'pregnancy'

Now this is a divine act, and this pregnancy and birth impart
immortality to a living being who is mortal.

—*Symposium*, 206d

Nietzsche was drawn to images of
pregnancy, a rather dubious attraction for a writer so pronounced in
his disgust with women.[1] The attendant (but not necessarily female)
emblems of procreation—fecundity, heredity, genealogy, paternity, maternity, generation—all assemble to create a heady presence in Nietzsche's aphorisms and arguments. It is a curious feature of these remarks
that they often seem 'un-sexed'. Nietzsche's pregnancies and deliveries
are, if anything, 'male' in their aspect. Nietzsche does not seem feminized
by his pregnancies of the spirit, and he is uninterested in gestation of the
usual, female, sort.[2] These metaphors are another expression of Nietzsche's deep philological commitments. He admires the classical notion
that sexuality and generation are tangible representatives of the entire
human economy of efflorescence and decline.

What did the Hellene guarantee to himself with these mysteries? *Eternal* life, the eternal recurrence of life; the future promised and conse-
crated in the past; the triumphant Yes to life beyond death and change;
true life as collective continuation of life through procreation, through

---

1. But it is not entirely clear what *sort* of misogynist Nietzsche was; for example, "Vergiss
die Peitsche nicht" is a remark made by a woman. Cf. R. Hinton Thomas's article "Nietzsche,
Women and the Whip," in his *Nietzsche in German Politics and Society, 1890-1918*
(Manchester: Manchester University Press, 1983).
2. Pace Derrida; more about his views momentarily.

[handwritten: PROOF THAT N's ETERNAL RETURN WAS NOT COSMOLOGICAL]

the mysteries of sexuality. It was for this reason that the *sexual* symbol
✱   was for the Greeks the symbol venerable as such.[3]

The most obvious classical antecedent of 'spiritual pregnancy' is Diotima's instruction of Socrates in the *Symposium*; in fact, Nietzsche makes
many oblique references to the dialogue.[4] It is useful to contrast Nietzschean pregnancy with Diotimean pregnancy and, as we outline these
similarities and differences, we might wonder why Nietzsche apparently
draws so close to the enemy, Plato, on this particular point.

Before this comparison can be drawn, however, I must distinguish my
concerns from those of Derrida and his commentators.[5] This chapter
raises the question of the 'mechanics', so to speak, of the pregnancy
metaphor, and does not raise the attendant query of what the use of this
metaphor 'means for woman', or what we may thus take Nietzsche to
believe about women, or even in what sense Nietzsche is 'feminized' by
this metaphor. My analysis begins with Diotima's extended image of
pregnancy (an emblem to which Nietzsche is enormously indebted) and
follows her procedure. Diotima's discussion of the many sorts of pregnancies, spiritual and physical, does not, of course, attempt to decode these
metaphors in order to understand what 'woman' is. In following this naive
program, I should point out that these images do raise such dangerous
questions, ones that seem to imperil any other reading of the metaphor.[6]

---

3. Nietzsche, "What I Owe to the Ancients," in *Twilight of the Idols* 4. This passage is
further indication that Nietzsche did not hold a cosmological view of eternal recurrence.

4. Kaufmann tells us that Nietzsche "stated in his curriculum vitae that Plato's *Symposium* was his *Lieblingsdichtung*" (*Nietzsche: Philosopher, Psychologist, Antichrist*, p. 23).

5. See, for example, Jacques Derrida, *Spurs/Eperons, Nietzsche's Styles/Les Styles de
Nietzsche*, trans. Barbara Harlow (Chicago: University of Chicago Press, 1979); and Derrida's
commentators, in particular Gayatri Spivak, "Displacement and the Discourse of Women,"
in *Displacement: Derrida and After*, ed. Mark Krupnick (Bloomington: Indiana University
Press, 1983); and David Farrell Krell, *Postponements: Women, Sensuality and Death in
Nietzsche* (Bloomington: Indiana University Press, 1986).

6. Alison Ainley's essay "'Ideal Selfishness': Nietzsche's Metaphor of Maternity" (in
Exceedingly Nietzsche, ed. Krell and Wood [Routledge and Kegan Paul, 1988]) is a good
example of just how risky such questions are. At the outset Ainley remarks, "The metaphors
of pregnancy inform Nietzsche's attitudes toward creativity. Yet, on the other hand, they
also have bearing on the metaphors of women. . . . In other places he suggests that the
relation of mother to child provides the potentiality of a re-thought ethical relation to
others" (p. 116). However, in sorting out the implications of the pregnancy metaphor
vis-à-vis our view of women, Ainley neglects to explain this new ethical relation until the
final sentence: "The metaphor of maternity may not be reducible entirely to a relation of
dominance — 'being a', 'Woman as mother' — but may express an attempt to give ear to the
potentialities of other, surprising voices" (p. 128). Ainley's initial project, that of examining

My treatment of the pregnancy metaphor does not psychoanalyze Nietzsche's intent; rather, it focuses on the essential ambiguity in our thinking about a pregnant person, and what this ambiguity indicates about the best life.

I

I begin by asking: how does one become spiritually pregnant? In the *Symposium*, Diotima claims that all humans are already pregnant in both the soul and the body, and that the arrival of beauty inspires the person to give birth.

> Therefore the role of the goddess of childbirth is played by beauty. And because of this, whenever something pregnant approaches the ugly, it shrinks into itself. . . . It holds back and carries the burden of what it has inside itself with pain. In fact, in the pregnant one, who is teeming with life, there is a violent fluttering before the beautiful, through which it will be released from the great pain of childbirth which it has.[7]

Nietzsche cites this passage in order to contradict Schopenhauer:

> Schopenhauer speaks of beauty with a melancholy ardor . . . because he sees in it a bridge upon which one may . . . acquire the thirst to pass over. . . . No less an authority than the divine Plato (— so Schopenhauer himself calls him) maintains a different thesis: that all

the 're-thought' ethical relation suggested by the maternal metaphor, becomes instead an assessment of the 'feminine' in Nietzsche's work; that is, the significance of female images in Nietzsche's metaphors. This chapter will not address the pregnancy metaphor in this way. Its central concern will be the blurred distinctions pregnancy suggests: what is the status of the mother? Of the fetus? What sorts of distinctions do we make in thinking about gestation, and why?

The attendant question of what Nietzsche's use of this image means for women, is an important issue that must be raised elsewhere. Nietzsche's remarks are obviously offensive and sexist. However, in giving some of his metaphors a 'neutral' account I am crediting Nietzsche's skills as an anti-metaphysician; as such Nietzsche would not raise 'the question of woman' any more than he would raise 'the question of man', since he rejects the existence of any essential account of *human being*. This tension between 'Nietzsche, the late nineteenth-century sexist male' and 'Nietzsche, the insistent anti-metaphysicist', who stands in opposition to the former, was a concern of Chapter 2.

7. Plato, *Symposium* 206d – e, trans. Suzy Q. Groden, ed. John Brentlinger (Amherst: University of Massachusetts Press, 1970).

beauty incites to procreation — that precisely this is the *proprium* of its effect, from the most sensual regions up into the most spiritual.[8]

Nietzsche asserts that the presence of beauty elicits the creative response:

> Whenever man feels in any way depressed, he senses the proximity of something 'ugly'. His feeling of power, his will to power, his courage, his pride — they decline with the ugly, they increase with the beautiful.[9]

Nietzsche also thinks that some human beings are 'maternal types',[10] that they are fruitful by their very nature, and that beauty will draw these fruits from them. Nietzsche is usually pleased to note the way in which things great and beautiful spur human action. *Daybreak* 76 praises Eros and Aphrodite as being "great powers capable of idealization." Similarly, Nietzsche is enthusiastic about the French troubadours,[11] a tradition founded on the notion of an unobtainable love object on whose behalf one performs acts of valor.

> — Love as passion — it is our European specialty — absolutely must be of aristocratic origin: it was, as is well known, invented by the poet-knights of Provence, those splendid, inventive men of the *gai saber* to whom Europe owes so much and, indeed, almost itself.[12]

What then is the purpose of these spiritual pregnancies? What sort of progeny do they produce? Again, it is useful to think about the Platonic goal, which is more explicit than Nietzsche's. The Platonic goal of the lover ascending the ladder of beauty is *immortality*. Since "mortal nature always seeks as much as it can to exist forever and achieve immortality," and since it is able to accomplish this only through procreation,[13] the goal of the pursuit of the beloved is not simply the beloved person, but immortality through procreation in the beautiful. "It is this very thing, Socrates,

---

8. Nietzsche, *Twilight of the Idols* 22.

9. Ibid., 20.

10. Nietzsche, *The Gay Science* 376: "This is how all artists and people of 'works' feel, the motherly, human type: at every division of their lives which are always divided by a work, they believe that they have reached their goal."

11. The troubadours are also mentioned in *Beyond Good and Evil, Twilight of the Idols, The Gay Science,* and *Ecce Homo.*

12. Nietzsche, *Beyond Good and Evil* 260.

13. Plato, *Symposium* 207d.

for the sake of which all the earlier hardships were suffered."[14] When the lover finally beholds the "great sea of beauty"[15] he may put aside his spiritual pregnancies. "Only there, seeing in the way that the Beautiful can be seen, can one stop giving birth to images of virtue . . . because one now grasps the truth." Diotima concludes that "if any man can be immortal, it will be he."[16]

We may also pose this question for Nietzsche: what is the goal of these pregnancies? What progeny do they produce, and how is that progeny connected to the pregnancy that produced it? Nietzsche often expresses his devotion to a goal. "Formula of our happiness: a Yes, a No, a straight line, a goal."[17] This goal is the beautifully crafted *thought*. "We philosophers . . . have to give birth to our thoughts out of pain and, like mothers, endow them with all we have of blood, heart, fire, pleasure, passion, agony, conscience, fate and catastrophe."[18] As with human childbirth, a thought is 'born' when it wants;[19] it must be continually 'brooded over',[20] and a good conversation is in fact the process of each serving as 'midwife' for the interlocutor.[21] Indeed, only true thinkers suffer this sort of pregnancy, and can be recognized accordingly.[22] Eternal joy, for this thinker, is the torment of spiritual childbirth.[23]

These 'thought-progeny' are, of course, not simply any collection of malformed, half-baked ideas. These thoughts must be, in their aspect, *immortal*, or we are instructed to destroy them.

> A man who held a newborn child in his hands approached a holy man. 'What shall I do with this child?' he asked; 'it is wretched, misshapen, and does not have life enough to die.' 'Kill it!' shouted the holy man with a terrible voice; 'and then hold it in your arms for three days and three nights to create a memory for yourself: never again will you beget a child when it is not time for you to beget.'[24]

---

14. Ibid., 211.
15. Ibid., 210d.
16. Ibid., 212.
17. Nietzsche, *The Anti-Christ* 1; cf. "Maxims and Arrows," in *Twilight of the Idols* 44.
18. Nietzsche, *The Gay Science*, Preface 3 — We might also note that the 'children' produced by spiritual pregnancies are, literally, articulate, while the one who is pregnant is accordingly 'speechless' (as in *Daybreak* 177).
19. Nietzsche, *Beyond Good and Evil* 17.
20. Nietzsche, *The Gay Science* 381.
21. Nietzsche, *Beyond Good and Evil* 136.
22. Ibid., 206; also 292.
23. Nietzsche, "What I Owe to The Ancients," in *Twilight of the Idols* 4.
24. Nietzsche, *The Gay Science* 73; also *Assorted Opinions and Maxims* 216: "There are

An immortal idea is characterized, above all, by its liveliness.

> I too have been in the underworld, like Odysseus, and will often be
> there again. . . . There have been four pairs who did not refuse
> themselves to me . . .: Epicurus and Montaigne, Goethe and Spinoza,
> Plato and Rousseau, Pascal and Schopenhauer. With these I have had to
> come to terms when I have wandered long alone, from them will I
> accept judgment, to them I will listen when in doing so they judge one
> another. . . . May the living forgive me if they sometimes appear to
> me as shades, so pale and ill-humored, so restless and alas! so lusting for
> life: whereas those others then seem to me so alive, as though now,
> after death, they could never again grow weary of life. *Eternal liveli-*
> *ness, however, is what counts: what do eternal life, or life at all,*
> *matter to us!*[25]

These 'works of liveliness' acquire their own sort of life;

> *The book become almost human.* — Every writer is surprised anew
> how, once a book has detached itself from him, it goes on to live a life
> of its own; it is to him as though a part of an insect had come free and
> was now going its own way . . . perhaps he no longer even under-
> stands it and has lost those wings upon which he flew when he
> thought out the book: during which time it seeks out its readers,
> enkindles life . . . in short, it lives like a being furnished with soul
> and spirit and is yet not human.[26]

This important passage ends with the remark:

> If one now goes on to consider that, not only in a book, but every
> action performed by a human being becomes in some way the cause of
> other actions, decisions, thoughts, that everything that happens is
> inextricably knotted to everything that will happen, one comes to
> recognize the existence of an *actual immortality*, that of motion

---

highly gifted spirits who are always unfruitful simply because, from a weakness in their
temperament, they are too impatient to wait out the term of their pregnancy."

25. Nietzsche, *Assorted Opinions and Maxims* 408; additional emphasis mine. It is
indeed liveliness that is the positive element in question, and not content: Nietzsche fires
vicious salvos at all of these thinkers at one time or another (though rarely at Goethe).

26. Nietzsche, *Human, All Too Human* 208; I have altered the translation ("sobald es
sich von ihm gelöst hat").

(Bewegung): what has once moved is enclosed and eternalized in the total union of all being like an insect in amber.[27]

Every act is 'knotted' to every other, but only the 'liveliest' of acts, thoughts, and lives will engender an abundance of other acts, thoughts, and lives. Once again, the immortal thoughts that have moved the thinker are captured in the midst of their movement. The words on the page or the paint on the canvas do not change,[28] but the sympathetic audience will see these works in 'mid-expression', and will thus be affected by them.

Obviously, even a 'spiritual' pregnancy must be prompted by some external force, and greeted by a corresponding necessary receptiveness:[29] a person must be moved by something other, something discrete from himself. This receptivity is a dangerous, vulnerable state. In the *Symposium* these dangers are hinted at in Diotima's description of the soul's ascent through different love attachments:

> It is necessary . . . to begin as a young man by being drawn to the beauty of the body, and if he is being guided properly by his guide, to love the beauty of one body, and for the fruit of this love to be beautiful conversations. But then this man must perceive that the beauty of one particular body is related to the beauty of another body, and if he must pursue beauty of form it is utterly senseless not to consider as one and the same the beauty which exists in all bodies. Once he has understood this, he will become a lover of all beautiful bodies, but he'll despise his lust for the one, and give it up, considering it petty.[30]

But what if the lover in question does not make this generalizing move, and continues to fixate on the beloved, particular person?[31] Then there can be no ascension through the various forms of beauty, and thus no ultimate view of the Beautiful. Diotima remarks that the "correct use of his love for

---

27. Ibid.; emphasis mine.

28. Although paintings do suffer more than books in this regard.

29. In *The Gay Science* 72, Nietzsche makes an unfortunate alliance between his own misogynist view of women and his more interesting account of spiritual pregnancy: "Pregnancy has made women kinder, more patient, more timid, more pleased to submit, and just so does spiritual pregnancy produce the contemplative type."

30. Plato, *Symposium* 210b.

31. Alcibiades seems to be an instance of this mistake; many commentators have made this point, including Martha Nussbaum in *The Fragility of Goodness* (Cambridge: Cambridge University Press, 1986); and Michael Garagin in his article "Socrates' *Hybris* and Alcibiades' Failure," *Phoenix* 31, no. 1 (1977): 22–37.

boys"[32] will lead the lover to the Beautiful itself, but an incorrect love will see the beloved person as an end in himself.

Nietzsche also thinks that the receptivity demanded by spiritual pregnancy is perilous, but for different reasons. An artist, in order to create, must be receptive to more than just the presence of beauty; he must be sensitive to many forces at work in the culture. In striving toward a particular artistic goal, the artist, the writer, must not set himself apart from 'average everydayness'.

> The study of the average human being, protracted, serious, and with much dissembling, self-overcoming, intimacy, bad company—all company is bad company except the company of one's equals—: this constitutes a necessary part of the life story of every philosopher.

But the creator is therefore drawn into habits and concerns that could undermine his creativity, or the 'will to create'. Nietzsche claims that, although superior human beings will want to remain 'as citadels', they must resist this impulse, for knowledge requires involvement. "If he continually avoids it and . . . remains hidden quietly and proudly away . . . then one thing is sure: he is not made, he is not predestined for knowledge."[33] This recommendation, although intuitively obvious, is a strange one for Nietzsche, the champion and defender of the philosopher's solitude. Only a few sections later in *Beyond Good and Evil*, Nietzsche makes a more characteristic observation: "We are born, sworn friends of solitude, of our own deepest, most midnight, most midday solitude — such a type of man are we, we free spirits!"[34] If solitude is the philosopher's haven, why must he engage in continual commerce with those who will least respect and appreciate the philosopher's task? What is the point of this trafficking with the resentful, the malformed, the leveled, the Christian, the democratic?

The creator's engagement with his cultural environment is crucial, not as a good in itself, but because becoming involved with other people, by intiating projects and working in their interest, an artist is provided with material for creation. "Poets behave impudently towards their experiences: they exploit them."[35] An artist must draw from her life experiences

---

32. Plato, *Symposium* 211c.

33. Nietzsche, *Beyond Good and Evil* 273. This 'necessity' is reminiscent of the ambiguous necessity of the higher men in *Zarathustra*.

34. Nietzsche, *Beyond Good and Evil* 44; note the familiar presence of noontide.

35. Nietzsche, *Beyond Good and Evil* 161.

and transform them into art: that is how a person 'overcomes' those experiences.

> Out of this feeling (of intoxication) one gives to things, one compels them to take, one rapes them — one calls this process idealizing. Let us get rid of a prejudice here: idealization does not consist, as is commonly believed, in a subtracting or deducting of the petty and the secondary. . . . In this condition one enriches everything out of one's own abundance: what one sees, what one desires, one sees swollen, strong, overladen with energy. The man in this condition transforms things until they mirror his power — until they are reflections of his perfection. *This compulsion to transform into the perfect is — art.*[36]

The artist thus violently impregnates (viz., 'rapes') his own experiences. By dwelling on his private grievances and torments the artist bestows them with a transforming vitality that, in turn, the work of art (hopefully) communicates. In this sense the artist may even be grateful for these torments:

> *And become bright again.* — We openhanded and rich in spirit, standing by the road like open wells with no intention to fend off anyone who feels like drawing from us — we unfortunately do not know how to defend ourselves when we want to: we have no way of preventing people from darkening us: the time in which we live throws into us that which is most timebound; its dirty birds drop their filth into us; boys their gew-gaws; and exhausted wanderers their little and large miseries. But we shall do what we have always done: whatever one casts into us, we take down into our depth — for we are deep, we do not forget — *and become bright again.*[37]

I quote this passage in full for its analogies to impregnation. The artist, as free spirit, is an 'open well' into which the exigencies of life are dropped. The free spirit knows the alchemical secret of the spirit, however, and he is able to transmute that dross into a work of art. Nietzsche is again his own best example. In the Preface to *Ecce Homo* he remarks, "How should I not

---

36. Nietzsche, "Expeditions of an Untimely Man," in *Twilight of the Idols* 8 and 9; emphasis mine.

37. Nietzsche, *The Gay Science* 378; cf. *Assorted Opinions and Maxims* 332: "We would let nothing perish unused and see in every event, thing and man welcome manure, rain, sunshine."

be grateful to my whole life?" — a gratitude that does not distinguish his personal torments from the writings that they inspired and informed.

Diotima sees a person's loves as a *means* of glimpsing the Beautiful; similarly, Nietzsche is drawn to an account that may fairly be called an 'instrumental' understanding of a person's passions and interests. Those who are 'openhanded and rich in spirit' will view their disappointments, detractors, and even their successes as material to come to terms with through the transformation of art. The best of these transformations will stand as 'immortal' artworks, which will generate thoughtful praise and criticism and will the artist into forming other works. The comparison with Plato is striking. Rather than producing immortal souls, Nietzsche proposes that we produce immortal thoughts. There is a further similarity: the immortality of the individual, corporeal human being is, naturally, a matter of indifference; it is the business of that temporal, fleshy existence to make the immortality of its soul, or its work, possible.[38] This scheme does not seem to leave room for anything singular or blessed, for any relationship or event that is not treated as interpretive material.

Nietzsche knew that the free-spirited attitude presented this difficulty. In *The Wanderer and His Shadow* 301, he remarks, "Someone said: 'There are two people upon whom I have never thoroughly reflected: it is the testimony to my love for them.'" The way in which reflection dismantles everything it investigates is a problem I discussed in Chapter 2. The object there was to determine how we could maintain a set of ethical views in a reflective milieu, but here reflection emerges as an erotic issue: how can a lover resist 'overcoming' his erotic attachment? Zarathustra's loves, we should remember, *always* end by his opposing them. In *The Gay Science* Nietzsche recounts how it is that the habits, things, and even people in his life are supplanted.

> I love brief habits and consider them as an inestimable means for getting to know many things and states. . . . My nature is designed entirely for brief habits . . . I always believe that here is something that will give me lasting satisfaction — *brief habits, too, have this faith of passion, this faith in eternity . . . and now it nourishes me at noon* and in the evening and spreads a deep contentment all around itself. . . . But one day its time is up; the good thing parts from me. . . . Even then something new is waiting at the door, along with

---

38. Unlike Plato, however, the liveliness of the work in question fulfills no moral requirements: it is sufficient that it be lively and independent, that the role it plays in its cultural setting is vivid and singular.

my faith — this indestructible fool and sage! — that this new discovery will be just right, and that this will be the last time. This what happens to me with dishes, ideas, human beings, cities, poems, music, doctrines, ways of arranging the day, and life styles.[39]

Each attraction bears the faith that it will be the answer to a particular need, yet each in its turn is overcome, only to be replaced with a new piece of faith. Only one love is exempt from this inevitable cycle of acceptance and opposition. One love *is* an end in itself; I shall examine it at the end of this chapter.

We are now far from the usual account of Nietzsche's commitment to a kind of life termed 'Dionysian', a life that champions the importance of ecstatic union and the associated cycles of decay and renewal. Instead of joyous abandon for its own sake, our present account reveals a remarkably 'principled' abandon. The (Dionysian) circle of destruction and renewal is no longer the self-effacing joy that one might initially, and quite reasonably, assume it to be. Now we may perhaps conclude that the destructive acts of the free spirits are not wanton, but calculated, and that this destruction is by design. Zarathustra's definition of personal salvation shows as much. "To redeem the past and to transform every 'It was' into an 'I wanted it thus!' — that alone would I call redemption." The free spirits are perpetually caught up in this interpretive task; no experience may stand free of this reflective undertaking. How then can the free spirit embrace anything wholeheartedly?

Platonic and Nietzschean immortality both suggest *self-sufficiency*: the immortal soul who sees the Beautiful no longer needs individual, particular beautiful persons and acts to stimulate him. Similarly, the immortal thought is stung into being by some external word, act, or accident, but the thought, once formulated, no longer needs the situation that created it. The author, who is prompted to her remarks by various occasions, incidents, intrusions, produces something that is ultimately able to stand apart from whatever originally fostered it. That lively thought is self-sufficient, like the insect in amber. *"How one ought to turn to stone. —*Slowly, slowly to become hard like a precious stone — and at last to lie there, silent and a joy to eternity."[40] Of course, it is not the thinker herself who 'turns to stone', but her 'thought- children'; paradoxically, their hardness is not a symbol of stasis but an immortal reminder of their 'movement', as, say, the figures on Keats's krater are perpetually in motion.

---

39. Nietzsche, *The Gay Science* 295; emphasis mine.
40. Nietzsche, *Daybreak* 541.

The self-sufficiency indicated by Nietzsche's 'thought-progeny' is the independence of the work of art, and is thus different from the Platonic rejection of the particular. Nietzschean self-sufficiency is the sort borne out by every great creative work. Just as the new mother suppresses "the repellent and bizarre aspects of pregnancy, which . . . must be forgotten if one is to enjoy the child,"[41] so too the 'child' must detach itself from its antecedents in order to be a fully developed, 'immortal' thought. This thought must be able to stand free of its origins, perhaps even stand as a rebuke to its origins.

The child is a tremendously potent figure in Nietzsche's cast of characters. Though aphorisms about child's play and childlike imaginings are common, the most famous appearance of this trope is, of course, the child of the *Three Metamorphoses*. Here again is Nietzsche's curious emblem of the highest life:

> The child is innocence and forgetfulness, a new beginning, a sport, a self-propelling wheel, a first motion, a sacred Yes. Yes, a sacred yes is needed, my brothers, for the sport of creation: the spirit now wills its own will, the spirit sundered from the world now wins *its own* world.

The highest incarnation of spirit is the child, but, as we have seen, it is a baffling directive. As Gadamer points out, how can we will the innocence of the child?[42] The child is a puzzling model of the best kind of life, but better sense can be made of it if we focus on (as the passage urges us to do) the act of creation. So viewed, the child is an image of the work of art as well as a description of the creative process.

It is intriguing that the child of *The Three Metamorphoses* suggests the artist who creates as well as the artwork created. As the child is absorbed in his game, so the artist becomes absorbed in her creation. The child as the newly won world, however, bears a greater resemblance to the artistic product. The 'new world' is the product of the creative act, and it is a space of shapes, forms, ideas, or characters that the artist (and those who follow her work) can enter at will. It is an important feature of this 'Zarathustran child' that it has this double sense of being at the same time both creator and creation,[43] and thus suggestive of two different kinds of self-sufficiency. I shall come back to this doubleness later in this chapter.

---

41. Nietzsche, *The Genealogy of Morals*, Essay III 4.

42. Hans-Georg Gadamer, "The Drama of Zarathustra," in *Nietzsche's New Seas*, p. 222.

43. Cf. *Beyond Good and Evil* 225: "In man creature and creator are united . . . do you understand this antithesis?"

II

I should summarize my comparison thus far. Both Nietzsche and Diotima exhort us toward an instrumental view of our undertakings. For Diotima, a person engages in his activities in order to have an immortal soul, while in Nietzsche's case it is for the sake of an immortal work, and each of these ends has its own kind of autonomy. An immortal, gemlike, self-sufficient thought or work is evidently the goal of Nietzsche's spiritual pregnancy. But this is a bizarre conclusion, for more than one reason. Why would Nietzsche, an advocate of Dionysian abandon and frenzy, find no value in the activities themselves? Why would Nietzsche, the archgenealogist who specializes in unmasking practices and revealing the untidy and sordid origins of our beliefs, promote an end that denies and conceals its antecedents?

Before these questions can be answered, however, I must complete my examination with another Platonic analogy. Even Diotima's description, in fact (in the context of Plato's late works), is not the end of the story. In the *Phaedrus*, Plato provides an alternative to the ascent of eros described in the *Symposium*. In light of this more human outlook on eros, perhaps Diotima's account of eros should be reconsidered.

The *Phaedrus* takes place in that setting that especially, as we have seen, evokes the Übermensch, the environs of Pan[44] — certainly a dangerous place for Socrates and Phaedrus to be, even more so at Pan's sacred hour of the day, noon.[45] The Panic madness[46] suggested by this setting is further invoked by Socrates' claims about eros. Now, instead of being a means of immortality, eros is one of the four types of divine madness, and to be repected as such.

> 'False is the tale' that when a lover is at hand favour ought rather to be accorded to one who does not love, on the ground that the former is mad, and the latter sound of mind. That would be right if it were an invariable truth that madness is an evil: but in reality, the greatest

---

44. Cf. *The Wanderer and His Shadow* 308 and the connection between Mittag and the Augenblick in which the Übermensch comes into being.

45. Nussbaum makes this observation in *The Fragility of Goodness*, p. 200.

46. Which, as always, is ambiguous. The presence of Pan is *both* the promise of seduction or the threat of terror, which is perhaps why Socrates gives such a careful account of the different varieties of madness, benevolent and otherwise. Patricia Merivale provides a useful survey of the figure of Pan and its uses in her book *Pan the Goat-God* (Cambridge: Harvard University Press, 1969).

blessings come by way of madness, especially of madness that is heaven-sent.[47]

In *The Fragility of Goodness* Nussbaum begins her essay on the *Phaedrus* by setting forth two claims about the dialogue: some varieties of madness are required for insight and stability, and "erotic relationships of long duration between particular individuals (who see each other as such) are argued to be fundamental to psychological development and an important component of the best human life."[48] Neither of these claims belongs with Diotima's account of love. In the *Symposium* the madness associated with eros, the lover's passion for the beloved, is useful only insofar as it does not subvert the lover from pursuing the Beautiful itself, and certainly such passion was not a good 'in itself'. The *Phaedrus*, however, describes an erotic attachment between two persons that is good precisely because it does *not* generate a more detached perspective: the relationship of these lovers, and the feelings that unite them, are noninstrumental goods.[49]

The divine madness involved in this dialogue is a celebration of particular, corporeal beauty and its unique ability to stir the soul.

> This is the best of all forms of divine possession, both in itself and in its sources, both for him who has it and for him who shares therein; and when he that loves beauty is touched by such madness he is called a lover. Such a one, as soon as he beholds the beauty of this world, is reminded of true beauty.[50]

A person does not set out to have such attachments; rather, that person is overtaken by them.[51] Even though this passion for another does have the

---

47. Plato, *Phaedrus*, trans. R. Hackforth (Cambridge: Cambridge University Press, 1952), 244b.

48. Nussbaum, *The Fragility of Goodness*, p. 201.

49. Giovanni Ferrari remarks:

> The story in the Phaedrus is significantly different in that Socrates focuses on the joint development of a loving couple . . . over the course of a lifetime. . . . Diotima on the development of a single individual — which, moreover, she narrates as an emancipation from concern for the beauty (physical or spiritual) of any other individual.

Listening to the Cicadas (Cambridge: Cambridge University Press, 1988), pp. 170–71.

50. Plato, *Phaedrus* 249d–e.

51. E. R. Dodds makes this observation: "[This fourth sort of madness] was a 'given', something that happens to a man without his choosing it or knowing why—the work, therefore, of a formidable daemon" ("Plato and the Irrational Soul," *Plato II*, ed. Gregory

effect of awakening the immortal part of a person, that effect does not diminish the importance of the relationship that created it.

> And now that he has come to welcome his lover and to take pleasure in his company and converse, it comes home to him what a depth of kindliness he has found, and he is filled with amazement, for he perceives that all his other friends and kinsmen have nothing to offer in comparison with this friend in whom there dwells a god. . . . These then, my dear boy, are the blessings great and glorious which will come to you from the friendship of a lover.[52]

Lest we forget the origins of this sort of madness, Socrates directs a prayer to Pan at the end of the dialogue.[53]

There are now two models for the workings of eros. According to Diotima, love is that which prompts us to form attachments and follow artistic and political pursuits, with the view of the Good itself as the goal of these attachments. The *Phaedrus* reminds us that loving relationships are a divine madness and a boon in their own right.[54] Questions may now be posed of Nietzsche's writings: does he recommend a comparable 'Diony-sian', 'Panic' playfulness for its own sake? Can we view Nietzsche's own use of this Panic imagery and metaphor as an analogous response to his own more extreme account of immortality?

If we can, then it seems that we have returned to the opposition we were left with in *Zarathustra*, namely, the perfect, finished Übermensch of the Augenblick standing as the epiphanic response to the sufferings and lacunae of self-overcoming. The split seems inevitable. Nietzsche deni-grates the suffering of the free spirits, and fixes his gaze on the immortal thoughts and works that such suffering might produce. Yet he also offers us the Panic images of self-dissolution; a joyful, redemptive frenzy that serves no ends whatsover, and the Augenblick, the noontide repose that must be its own end, complete in itself.

Vlastos [Notre Dame: University of Notre Dame Press, 1978], p. 220). This description is different from the rational ascent through progressively more abstract beauties in the *Symposium*.

52. Plato, *Phaedrus* 255b–256e.

53. Classicists are not in agreement about what the prayer means, however. For ex-ample, Diskin Clay, in "Socrates' Prayer to Pan" (in *Arktouros* [Berlin and New York: Walter de Gruyter, 1979]), claims that the prayer should also be heard as an invocation of Eros, whose daimonic presence (as in the *Symposium*) will connect him with the philosophic riches Socrates is requesting (in the form of a riddle) of Pan.

54. Toward this end we should note the contrast with Lysias's utterly instrumental view of relationships.

Is this dichotomy our final answer? Are the free spirits destined to swing back and forth between these two poles? If we follow the Platonic analogy, we should not expect a single answer from Nietzsche. Plato scholars do not expect the dialogues to give a univocal view, and many issues must remain unsettled. For example, in the *Symposium*, Diotima tells us that Eros is not a god, but a daemon existing between the gods and mortals; in the *Phaedrus*, however, Socrates claims that Eros is a great god, to whom he must now offer his apologies. Perhaps we must take the same approach with Nietzsche, and accept the presence of incompatible views, and incompatible instructions about the best life to lead.

But before we resign ourselves to this dualism we should reconsider the metaphor of pregnancy. Our initial characterization overlooked an important metaphorical clue. The condition of being pregnant is treated in a way that contains an important ambiguity — one that, I suggest, should not be resolved, even though the interpreter is invariably tempted to resolve it. Indeed, Nietzsche occasionally urges us to *remain pregnant*: The state of spiritual pregnancy is *itself* a blessed condition. "[Pregnancy] is a state of consecration, in which one can and should live!"[55] Living in a blessed state of gestation is quite different than being pregnant *in order to* bear a child. This ambiguous treatment corresponds to a similar confusion in the *Symposium* about pregnancy. At one point Diotima indicates that it is the condition of being pregnant that is valuable, not the offspring of one's immortal soul. Ultimately, of course, pregnancy is rejected in favor of immortality.

Initially, Diotima tells us that it is through procreation that the mortal achieves immortality,[56] which suggests that it is being pregnant, the process of generation, that confers immortality. At the end of the ascension passage, however, Diotima remarks that the lover who sees the Beautiful will stop being pregnant, because it is in fact this view of the Beautiful that (may) grant him immortality. Diotima's remarks about the pursuit of immortality can be read in two ways: one becomes immortal through procreation, be it physical or spiritual (but the latter is obviously preferred by Diotima), or one becomes immortal through witnessing the Beautiful, which evidently can only happen by ascending through the various forms of erotic attachment. This ambiguity has been attacked by critics who see the second formulation as denigrating the force of a person's particular attachments: one loves them only in order to 'overcome' them.[57]

---

55. Nietzsche, *Daybreak* 552.
56. Plato, *Symposium* 208b.
57. For example, Luce Irigaray remarks:

This division in Diotima's program[58] highlights an interesting feature of Nietzsche's own pursuit of spiritual pregnancy. Diotima claims that the ultimate progeny of procreating in the Beautiful is the immortal soul. The state of the soul as it beholds the Beautiful is the goal. The ambiguity emerges when we try to specify the status of each individual act of procreation along the way: did the lover love that person or that deed for itself, or because it emblematized the promise of eternal beauty, and hence eternal life?

These difficulties in mind, we should attempt to fix, so far as we can, Nietzsche's all-too suggestive metaphor of spiritual pregnancy. Before we can do so, however, there are two questions to be faced that this metaphor raises. How are we to think of the moment of inspiration, the metaphorical impregnation? Is this the moment in which the creator is set toward a goal, or is it merely an ecstatic moment that is followed by the creative intent? Further, how should we regard the accomplished goal, the work of art?

First, the matter of inspiration: this question is addressed not only to the artist, but also to the person who is viewing a painting, listening to a cantata, or, more directly for our purposes, reading an aphorism. Nietzsche clearly intends his work both to move and to inspire (rather than to instruct and to improve), but only a good reader will have the right sort of response. What constitutes an inspired reading of an aphorism? Nietzsche often claims that he has little confidence in his own readership. "One thing is necessary above all if one is to practice reading as an art . . . something that has been unlearned most thoroughly: . . . rumination." He remarks that the aphorism is a particular problem for the reader. "An aphorism, properly stamped and molded, has not been 'deciphered' when it has simply been read; rather, one has then to begin its exegesis, for which is required an art of exegesis." As for the book, *Also sprach Zarathustra*:

> I do not allow that anyone knows it who has not at some times been *profoundly wounded* and at some time *profoundly delighted* by every

---

[Diotima] leads love into a schism between mortal and immortal. Love loses its demonic character. . . . The perpetual passage from mortal to immortal that lovers confer on one another is put aside. . . . A beloved who is a will, even a duty, and a means of attaining immortality. . . . Immortality is the object of their love. Not love itself.

"Sorcerer Love," *Hypatia* 3, no. 3 (1989): 32–44. Martha Nussbaum makes a similar observation in *The Fragility of Goodness*, p. 182.

58. I will not claim that Diotima does, or does not, actually give us two formulations; it is the possibility of these two readings and the sort of controversy this possibility creates that is helpful for our concerns.

word of it; for only then may he enjoy the halcyon element out of which that book was born and in its sunlight clarity, remoteness, breadth and certainty.[59]

A reader must first be open to the aphorism, then must be capable of being shocked or elated by it. The aphorism's 'charms' must first and foremost be allowed to take effect.[60] Hence Nietzsche's prohibitions about reading his maxims with the intention of "tracing the general observation back to the particular event to which the maxim owes its origin." A reader with this approach is comparable to a theatergoer who insists on sneaking backstage to look at the scenery and properties before the curtain goes up. We are required, just for a moment, to suspend our critical faculties; in this way the work of art can render its sublime effect. "What is essential in art remains its perfection of existence, its production of perfection and plenitude; art is essentially affirmation, blessing, deification of existence — What does a pessimistic art signify? Is it not a *contradictio*? — Yes."[61]

Obviously, this effect is fleeting. We may be inspired, awe-struck, thrilled, all in the "blink of an eye," but we are then faced with either the responsibility of rendering our vision in a creative work (if we are artists) or the equally arduous chore of understanding what has so moved us (if we are interpreters). The process of coming to terms with a work of art is the 'science of hermeneutics' on which Nietzsche always insists. A good theater critic, art historian, or reader of aphorisms must be capable of being filled with an inarticulate delight (impregnation, to follow the metaphor) that eventually flourishes as a thoughtful critique.[62] Inspiration, in order truly to be inspiration, must be a moment of unqualified delight, of self-effacement and abandon; however, it must *also*, that is, at the same time, be the spur toward the generation of something else. If it is not, we would be reluctant to call such a moment *inspiring* — joyful, perhaps, or narcotic, but not inspiring. 'Inspiration' implies the creation of something new from itself; paradoxically, its occurrence requires a certain inviolability and awe that does not allow for manipulation: a person cannot demand to be inspired in order to do something. Like the descent of Panic madness or the frenzy of Dionysus, its origins are external. Thus, inspiration is itself a

---

59. Nietzsche, *The Genealogy of Morals*, Preface, section 8; emphasis mine.

60. Cf. "The eye of Venus that charms and blinds even our opponents, the magic of the extreme" (*Will to Power* 749)

61. Ibid., 821.

62. It is a truism that readers who are not moved by Nietzsche's rhetorical displays are also hopeless at understanding him.

twofold proposition: one is 'overwhelmed' at the same time as one 'takes command' of an idea.

If we ask, further, how we may think of the completed work of art, we must think again about goals and their pursuit. Certainly, Zarathustra urges his audience to become focused on an ultimate goal: "Yet tell me my brothers: if a goal for humanity is still lacking, is there not still lacking — humanity itself?"[63] Zarathustra's goal is quite clear, and it is expressed in maternal terms: Zarathustra is interested in his 'children' (presumably Übermenschen), and not in either his audience or himself. "You are only bridges: may higher men than you step across upon you! . . . From your seed there may one day grow for me a genuine seed and perfect heir: but that is far ahead. You yourselves are not those to whom my heritage and name belong."[64] This attitude is familiar from Chapter 3: the free spirit engaged in self-overcoming denies his self as it is currently constituted and identifies himself with his goal. " 'I want heirs,' thus speaks everything that suffers,' 'I want children, I do not want myself.' Joy, however, does not want heirs or children, joy wants itself." As we discovered in that chapter, a goal so conceived of is, to say the least, problematic. A free spirit is thus only able to accept himself for brief, epiphanic moments that are opaque and unavailable from the perspective of self-overcoming. Other passages in *Zarathustra*, however, express a somewhat different understanding of the way in which goal and process are connected. In "On the Blissful Islands" Zarathustra remarks,

> For the creator himself to be the child new-born he must also be willing to be the mother and endure the mother's pain.
>
> Truly, I have gone my way through a hundred souls and through a hundred cradles and birth-pangs. I have taken many departures, I know the heart-breaking last hours.
>
> But my creative will, my destiny, wants it so. Or, to speak more honestly: my will wants precisely such a destiny.[65]

The creator, rather than yearning for a not-yet-existent child, now *is* the child, but only insofar as the creator is also able to accept the suffering he must endure through the creative process; that is, only insofar as he is capable of remaining pregnant. We may recall the child from the "Three

63. Nietzsche, "On the Thousand and One Goals," in *Thus Spake Zarathustra*, Part 1.
64. Nietzsche, "The Greeting," in *Zarathustra*, Part 4.
65. Nietzsche, "On the Blissful Islands," in *Zarathustra*, Part 2.

Metamorphoses" who "wins his own world." The artist who, in his creations, is *both* mother and child, is simultaneously self-possessed and given
over to something outside himself; he makes determinations while himself
being determined by the choices that constitute the world of his creation.

Pregnancy and overcoming are again conflated in "Of Self-Overcoming":

> And life told me this secret: 'Behold,' it said, 'I am that which must
> overcome itself again and again.'
>
> 'To be sure, you call it will to procreate or impulse towards a goal,
> towards the higher, more distant, more manifold: *but all this is one
> and one secret.*'

The 'will to procreate', the 'impulse toward a goal' is thus identified
with 'that which overcomes itself again and again' — an interesting notion
when we consider that these two activities are usually represented as
contradictions. Of course, in "The Intoxicated Song," Zarathustra marries
these attitudes: "Midnight is also noonday, pain is also joy, a curse is also a
blessing, the night is also a sun — be gone, or you will learn: a wise man is
also a fool." In Chapter 3 I attributed this list of identities to the perspective
of the Augenblick, the moment of joy, which embraces everything, including self-overcoming. Now we may offer a somewhat more prosaic reading,
namely, that the will to create is tied to the creation it envisions, and that
the final product owes its constitution to that creative process.

What sort of attitude toward a goal is Nietzsche thus recommending for
the free spirit? The individual is clearly instructed to pursue a higher, better
self, to have that better self as an end. Yet, as I have already noted in
Chapter 3, Nietzsche finds the notion of a goal problematic.

> I have learned to distinguish the cause of acting from the cause of
> acting in a particular way, in a particular direction, . . . with a par-
> ticular goal. The first kind of cause is a quantum of dammed-up energy
> that is waiting to be used up somehow . . . while the second kind is,
> compared to this energy, something quite insignificant, for the most
> part a little accident . . . a match versus a ton of powder. Among
> these little accidents and 'matches' I include so-called 'purposes' as
> well as the even more so-called 'vocations'. . . . The usual view is
> different: people are accustomed to consider the goal (purpose, voca-
> tion, etc.) as the *driving force* . . . but it is merely the *directing
> force* — one has mistaken the helmsman for the stream. . . . Is the
> 'goal', the 'purpose' not often enough a beautifying pretext, a

self-deception . . . that does not want to acknowledge that the ship is following the current into which it has entered accidentally? that it wills to go that way *because it — must?*[66]

A person's vocation is itself a self-deception, a 'piece of vanity' that masks much deeper, presumably cultural, forces that are at work. The desires and intentions that compose a person's character are in fact superficial indicators of deeper desires beyond the person's conscious intentions and desires. This conflict between what a person makes of herself and what makes up the person was the subject of Chapter 1. The resolution — if it counts as a resolution — is once again perspectival. A human being is a complex nexus of forces, a continuum of drives that cannot be given absolute coordinates. Whether or not a particular quality of a person is something the person has willed, or had willed upon them, is largely a matter of the question being posed, not of the quality itself, for there are no qualities 'an sich'.

Our first consideration of a 'goal' reveals the need for a thoroughgoing skepticism: any consciously chosen pursuit is only a preliminary indicator of what that person wants, or, to paraphrase Deleuze, what 'wants' the person.[67] Furthermore, a free spirit who has not yet asked himself *why* he must overthrow the requirements of the *nomos* is not yet critical enough, and has only a rudimentary understanding of his revolutionary goals.

In *The Wanderer and His Shadow* Nietzsche includes a number of aphorisms about goals:

> *Pleasure tourists.* — They climb the hill like animals, stupid and perspiring: no one has told them there are beautiful views on the way.

> *End and goal.* — Not every end is a goal. The end of a melody is not its goal; but nonetheless, if the melody had not reached its end it would not have reached its goal either. A parable.[68]

These rather gentle (and almost New Age) observations are very different from the usual manic exhortations of Zarathustra, but they bear a resemblance to the remarks we just considered. These aphorisms, which seem somewhat simplistic, might be rendered as follows: rather than storming

---

66. Nietzsche, *The Gay Science* 360.
67. Deleuze, *Nietzsche and Philosophy*, pp. xi - xii.
68. Nietzsche, *The Wanderer and His Shadow* 202 and 204.

angrily toward his destiny, the free spirit should take pleasure in the creative process, enjoying the work as well as its rewards. But a deeper and more difficult reading is also available. The free spirit should enjoy creativity as such, not only because creative efforts can be enjoyed, but because focusing on the outcome of an endeavor is a *mistake*. It indicates that the free spirit believes that the goal will complete the process, when in fact the creative product only generates new projects. " 'Whatever I create and however much I love it — soon I have to oppose it and my love: thus will my will have it.' " There is no end to any endeavor, and only perspectival, intermediate ways of determining when one project has ended and another has begun. In other words, 'goal', like inspiration, contains a dual concern. The end in question must be that toward which a person's efforts are directed. Nietzsche will insist, however, that no end is complete in itself, and in order to pursue it a person must understand how his goal is part of many other designs, beyond the scope of his particular endeavor. It is the familiar Nietzschean paradox: for a person truly to have a goal that person must be able to see it as, in a sense, no goal at all. Once again we arrive at a dichotomy: just as the moment of inspiration necessarily has two aspects, so too does the 'child', or the goal, of the spiritual pregnancy. The 'child', understood as the work of art, is separate from, as well as dependent on, all that constituted it. Furthermore, this twofold relationship is also present in all the many interpretive accounts that this 'child' must bear.

At last we can draw some conclusions about the analogic use of the ascent passage in the *Symposium*. Note Nietzsche's own observations about the difficulties created by the character Zarathustra:

> The psychological problem in the type of Zarathustra is how he, who to an unheard-of degree says No, can nonetheless be the opposite of a spirit of denial; how he, a spirit bearing the heaviest of destinies, a fatality of a task, can nonetheless be the lightest and most opposite — Zarathustra is a dancer — : how he, who has . . . the most fearful insight into reality, who has thought the 'most abysmal thought', nonetheless finds in it no objection to existence.[69]

Zarathustra is the opposite of the spirit of denial because there is an end toward which he strives, and a love that he holds unconditionally as an end in itself, and that is *eternity*.

---

69. Nietzsche, "Thus Spake Zarathustra," in *Ecce Homo*, section 6.

HUME ✳

Never yet did I find the woman by whom I wanted children, unless it be this woman, whom I love: for I love you, O Eternity:
For I love you, O Eternity![70]

This is a strange goal, because it is empty: 'eternity' is the emblem of the infinite interpretations that a free spirit creates by tearing down existing ones and fashioning new ones. What Zarathustra loves unconditionally, the end to which he is able to say, unreservedly, 'Yes', is this vista of endless interpretation. The familiar metaphor from Chapter 2 reappears:

> In the horizon of the infinite. — We have left the land and have embarked. . . . Now little ship, look out! Beside you is the ocean: to be sure, it does not always roar, and at times it lies spread out like silk. . . . But hours will come when you will realize that it is infinite and that there is nothing more awesome than infinity.

The Nietzschean free spirit becomes 'spiritually pregnant', and suffers the whole cycle of renewal and death, in much the same way that a follower of Diotima does, namely, with his eyes on the immortal and the eternal. Of course — and this qualification is essential — Diotima's student believes that a glimpse of the Good in itself is possible, and that is why he eagerly surveys the sea of beauty before him.

> One turns and contemplates the great sea of beauty; one brings forth many beautiful and magnificent theories and thoughts in a fruitful philosophy, until, growing strong and thriving in this environment, he comprehends a certain kind of knowledge, which is of this kind of beauty.[71]

This sort of metaphysical completion is, of course, anathema to Nietzsche. What his free spirit ultimately surveys, and what he acknowledges, is not the sea of eternal beauty, but a sea of infinite interpretation.

> Everything is sea, sea, sea! — And whither then would we go? Would we cross the sea? Whither does this mighty longing draw us, this

---

70. Nietzsche, "The Seven Seals," in *Zarathustra*, Part 3.

71. Plato, *Symposium* 210e. Cf. David Hume's naturalized version of this in his essay "The Platonist": "The Divinity is a boundless ocean of bliss and glory: human minds are smaller streams, which, arising at first from this ocean, seek still, amid all their wanderings, to return to it, and to lose themselves in that immensity of perfection" (*Essays, Moral, Political and Literary* [Oxford: Oxford University Press, 1963], p. 157).

longing that is worth more than any pleasure? Why just in this direction, thither where all the suns of humanity have hitherto gone down? Will it perhaps be said of us one day that we too, steering westward, hoped to reach an India — but that it was our fate to be wrecked against infinity? Or, my brothers. Or? —

These final words of *Daybreak* could stand as the free spirit's own final words. Certainly, disjunction has been the hallmark of this chapter. We are left hanging on a possibility, the concluding interrogation mark a reminder of Nietzsche's unwavering devotion to the reflective turn of destruction and creation.

But still: how do we 'remain pregnant' while being the 'child at play'?

III

I concluded Chapter 3 by noting Nietzsche's fascination with the metaphor of noon and its accompanying promise of somnolence and threat of panolepsy. There I raised the obvious question: how can the rapture of 'des mythischen Mittags' be integrated with the suffering of constant self-overcoming? Having considered the dual Platonic parallel, we must conclude that the very impulse to synthesize these two dimensions of life is the central problem we face as interpreters. However, by refusing to conflate these two — and this point is crucial — we are *not* simply left with a life that endlessly moves back and forth between 'overcoming' and 'bliss'. Our final task is to characterize, if we can, a person that simultaneously enjoys both kinds of experience, and to explain how it is that Nietzsche's use of the image of the child and the notion of pregnancy presents a different option.

In thinking about a pregnant woman, we generally have two ways of viewing her status. We might think of her as the custodian of an unborn child, as a rational, autonomous maternal being who has complete control over her helpless charge. In this light, we see her as the maker of choices, the bearer of responsibility. Conversely, we may see her as one who has been invaded, impregnated, her hormones and her life held hostage by a powerful, unknown homunculus, her autonomy undermined, and her very life dictated by forces beyond her control. The description need not be pejorative. We could follow Nietzsche's own example and see it as a mysterious, ecstatic loss of self. *Daybreak* 552 captures this 'double vision' of pregnancy:

Is there a more holy condition than pregnancy? To do all we do in the unspoken belief that it has somehow to benefit that which is coming to be within us! . . . In this condition we avoid many things without having to force ourself very hard! We suppress our anger, we offer the hand of conciliation: our child shall grow out of all that is gentlest and best. . . . *At the same time, a pure and purifying feeling of profound irresponsibility* reigns in us almost like that of the auditor before the curtain has gone up — *it* is growing, it is coming to light: we have no right to determine either its value or the hour of its coming. (Emphasis mine)

Julia Kristeva's remarks about pregnancy are relevant here. Kristeva proposes a new approach to ethical questions, called 'herethics'. Kelly Oliver describes this ethic as "founded on the relationship between mother and child during pregnancy and birth . . . *it is founded on the ambiguity in pregnancy and birth between subject and object positions.*"[72] Kristeva's psychoanalytic account of a maternal ethic is far from our own concerns, but her emphasis on the indeterminacy of the mother's status is instructive. In *Daybreak* 552, the pregnant person is in charge of the pregnancy, yet *also* divinely out of control, joyfully submitting to forces beyond the scope of choice or deliberation. In this sense the mother's autonomy is compromised. The challenge to the mother's autonomy is the result of the indistinct configuration in question: a pregnant body is simultaneously single and dual. We might say that a pregnancy involves two distinct entities that are remarkably blurred; on the other hand, we can describe the pregnant person as having two parts, the bearer and that which is borne, and conclude that this is an interesting duality,

---

72. Kelly Oliver, *Reading Kristeva: Unraveling the Double-Bind* (Bloomington: Indiana University Press), p. 66; emphasis mine. Kristeva's own enigmatic description of 'herethics' is as follows:

Now, if a contemporary ethics is no longer seen as being the same as morality; if ethics amounts to not avoiding the embarrassing and inevitable problematics of the law but giving it flesh . . . in that case its reformulation demands the contribution of women. Of women who harbor the desire to reproduce (to have stability). Of women who are available so that our speaking species, which knows it is mortal, might withstand death. Of mothers. For an heretical ethics separated from morality, an *herethics*, is perhaps no more than that which in life makes bonds, thoughts, and therefore the thought of death, bearable herethics is undeath.

Julia Kristeva, "Stabat Mater," in *Tales of Love*, trans. Leon Roudiez (New York: Columbia University Press, 1987), pp. 262–63.

since it requires that we acknowledge 'two' while treating them as somehow 'one'.

This necessarily indeterminate metaphor is the ultimate emblem of Nietzsche's model of the self, which is both active and receptive. More important, it is also his metaphor for the ideal life. An ideal life will have autonomy, responsibility, choice, and above all, lively critical faculties. However, that life must, *at the same time*, also recognize its manifold debts: to parenting, to its teachers, culture, language, and civilization. An ideal life will see itself as carrying forth imperatives that it did not create and that it cannot resolve, perhaps that it cannot even understand.

How, then, is this conjunction different from the two sorts of experience outlined in Chapter 3? *Indeed, it is the notion of pregnancy itself that conjoins, but does not conflate, self-overcoming and ecstatic self-effacement.* By urging us to 'remain pregnant', Nietzsche is attempting to create a viable hybrid of Zarathustra's dual teachings, an attempt that can be understood as a response to the differences between what we have identified as the *Symposium/Phaedrus* accounts of eros. Zarathustra's mistake now becomes clear. Zarathustra is unable to combine these two notions of erotic attachment, and is thus condemned to diremption. His rabid interest in his 'children' neglects his own teaching, that the creator is *himself* the child newborn.[73] The child is not the completed act of self-overcoming, but the 'coming to be' of that self-overcoming. Zarathustra fails to distinguish his imagined child—a shining, perfect, distant, and nonexistent creature[74]—from the very real child of *The Three Metamorphoses*. It is *this* child, in the midst of his absorbing play, that is the metaphorical mate to 'perpetual pregnancy'.

What Zarathustra cannot acknowledge is that the metaphoric pair of the 'child' and 'pregnancy' diagnose the troubling opposition of 'noon' and 'shadow'. 'Noon' and 'the child at play' both suggest autonomy, a sundering from the world, a separateness that can only be momentarily maintained. Playtime is eventually intruded upon by the cares of the world, just as 'perfect noon' only lasts for an instant. The difference, however, is that the child can take something away from his absorbed play, but, as we have seen, Zarathustra cannot retain anything from the ecstasy of noon except the memory of it. Likewise, the image of 'pregnancy' is a life-affirming version of the 'shadow'. Both metaphors suggest duality, self and other; both the shadow and the fetus are passively conjoined with an active self.

---

73. Nietzsche, "On the Blissful Islands, " in *Zarathustra*, Part 2.

74. Nietzsche, "Of Involuntary Bliss," in *Zarathustra*, Part 3; see also "The Greeting," in *Zarathustra*, Part 4.

The fetus, however, is not simply a shifting reflection of the mother's body, as the shadow must be, but a creature with the potential for autonomous life. A fetus depends on, and is produced by, the mother, yet it also has its own ineluctable and opaque program of development.

What kind of a model of the ideal life can thus be attributed to Nietzsche? The nature of its indeterminacy, so described, sets this account apart from the standard explanations of Nietzsche's 'teachings'. Typically, interpreters describe a strong model of the ideal self or no model at all. Some readers of Nietzsche see him as giving an explicit model that governs our understanding of his multifarious and sometimes contradictory remarks about the highest human life. Heidegger's rapacious Übermensch, Nehamas's vigilant self-interpreter, and, more recent, Leslie Paul Thiele's heroic individual are good examples of this strategy. These accounts adopt a 'totalizing' approach to Nietzsche's texts: they read them with the understanding that a single directive, a coherent ideal, is there to be found.

My account bears a greater resemblance to those offered by Foucault and Derrida. Derrida, for example, believes that we illegitimately presuppose a context for Nietzsche's fragmentary remarks when we give them a determinate sense, and that no such determinate sense should be offered. Gary Shapiro[75] makes a similar anti-totalizing move in his claim that both 'agents' and 'objects' are effaced through Nietzsche's attack on the narrative structure.[76] My reading of Nietzsche's diagnosis also denies that his remarks can be gathered into a univocal view of the self and the ideal life. The individual he describes is both autonomous and surrendered, suffering and ecstatic, constituted by custom yet driven to displace those habitual behaviors. The metaphors Nietzsche chooses are irreducibly opposed, yet fruitfully so. My version of Nietzsche's model of the self retains these oppositions, but it is nonetheless a model and guide. The 'ever-pregnant' person stands as some sort of model, despite its strangeness.

What else can we say about 'constant pregnancy'? Can this directive be made any clearer? We might remark (as my fellow female colleagues have done) that only a man could think that being permanently pregnant is a

---

75. Gary Shapiro, *Nietzschean Narratives* (Bloomington: Indiana University Press, 1989).

76. 'Noon' can be understood as either some sort of transcendental embrace or the advent of oblivion; regardless of how it is understood, no *absolute* sense can be attributed to this *Abgrund*. The 'genetic resemblance' between the Panic noontide and the Derridean sorts of accounts is this indeterminacy: any distinctions or identifications exist only temporarily over this interpretive abyss.

good idea. Many works on Nietzsche have pursued this question, what it means to have a man propose — and in so doing masculinize — this female process. Kelly Oliver, in *Womanizing Nietzsche*, claims that this appropriation of the maternal function is a method of taming a painful and frightening experience by denying the necessity of birth. "The Übermensch . . . is eternally pregnant with himself, a great health who does not need to give birth to anything other; the creator without creations; the artist without works of art; life become creative; son become mother."[77] Luce Irigaray points out that the child Zarathustra loves is himself: "What is the one spinning eternally around saying 'yes' to? To his self/same. His child, for example, this same that he has always wished to become. And he will have no other child."[78] In *Alcyone: Nietzsche on Gifts, Noise and Women*, Shapiro asserts that Nietzsche's pregnancies are hysterical, since he never gives birth.[79] These accounts emphasize Nietzsche's interest in creating himself, a self-absorption that has no interest in any other product. Nietzsche and his free spirits cannot acknowledge the potential separateness of that which they intend to bring to life.

Nietzsche's metaphor *does* appropriate and masculinize a female function, only honoring the male, 'spiritualized' version of it. In this sense the trope is not so different from Diotima's pregnancies, and her preference for giving birth to epic poems rather than to human infants. But there is more here than mere appropriation. Nietzsche is underlining one feature of being pregnant, one that remains a useful propaedeutic. Notice the emphasis in *Daybreak* 552, his most explicit comment on 'eternal pregnancy':

> 'What is growing here is something greater than we are' is our most secret hope: we prepare everything for it so that it may come happily into the world: not only everything that may prove useful to it but also the joyfulness and laurel-wreaths of our soul. —It is in this state of consecration that one should live! It is a state one can live in! And if what is expected is an idea, a deed — *towards every bringing forth we have no other relationship than that of pregnancy and ought to blow to the wind all presumptuous talk of 'willing' and 'creating'.* (Emphasis mine)

---

77. Oliver, *Reading Kristeva*, p. 146.

78. Luce Irigaray, *Marine Lover of Friedrich Nietzsche*, trans. Gillian Gill (New York: Columbia University Press, 1991), p. 15.

79. Gary Shapiro, *Alcyone: Nietzsche on Gifts, Noise and Women* (Albany: State University of New York Press, 1991), p. 136.

Nietzsche is questioning the scope of the creator's autonomy. Artists often have the conceit that, Prospero-like (indeed, Apollo-like) they arrange and place a created world before themselves. The metaphor of pregnancy underscores the limits of those creative powers. It is presumptuous, says Nietzsche, to focus on the activity of will when every creative act is indebted to forces at work in and on the artist. The best creative activity will not prize the power and clarity of its judgments more than the chthonic drives and visions that inspire artistic production. This metaphor does not venerate the supreme power of the will; rather, it recommends that we view our creative work with humility, even awe.

Nietzsche does not deny the 'births', the products of the free spirits, but he is calling our attention to the nature of creativity, much of which is beyond the artist's control, just as the biological program of the developing fetus is largely out of the mother's hands. The mother can take steps to ensure the health of the child, but these precautions are no guarantee of success. Fetal development depends on the mother, but ultimately it must make its own way. The artist can guide and shape her creation, but she depends on 'gifts' from within and from without. She must be inspired, and she must have a sense of the integrity, the wholeness of the things she shapes.

The 1886 preface to *Human, All Too Human* makes Nietzsche's intent clear:

> The secret force and necessity of this task will rule among and in the individual facets of his destiny like an unconscious pregnancy — long before he has caught sight of this task itself or knows its name. *Our vocation commands and disposes of us even when we do not yet know it*; it is the future that regulates our today . . . it is only now, *at the noontide of our life*, that we understand what preparations, bypaths, experiments, temptations, disguises the problem had need of *before it was allowed to rise up before us*, and how we first had to experience the most manifold and contradictory states of joy and distress in soul and body. (Emphasis mine)

The person living the highest life will renounce the lie of absolute autonomy; he will admit that the authority of his judgments is never a settled matter. He will acknowledge that a person is more constituted than constituting, and that human beings are joined and wedded to each other in ways that they must struggle to understand. His creations, his artworks, his writings, his children, are given to him, even as he works on them. In 'remaining pregnant', a person remains mindful that every act of creation, even at its completion, is the occasion for recognizing that other ideas have always already taken root within him. The work is complete, yet the worker is not.

The ideal life embodies the doubleness I have described and with ease, just as the pregnant woman just *is* one who is two. The spiritually pregnant individual is simply enduring a necessary means to an independent, autonomous, immortal child, yet that same individual is also, in her very being, a celebrant of this in-dwelling, this 'noontide' inspiration of the god. Just as the moment of inspiration is both a joyful end in itself as well as the beginning of future struggles and overcomings, so too is the mythical noontide a duality that is (somehow) not dual. The embrace of all things in the Augenblick is also apparently their division, yet one that does not truly divide.

> This song is done — desire's sweet cry died on the lips: a sorcerer did it, the timely friend, the noontide friend — no! ask not who he is — at noontide it happened, at noon one became two.[80]

---

80. Nietzsche, "From High Mountains: Epode," in *Beyond Good and Evil*.

References

All bibliographic information for works cited in this book is included in the footnotes.

All quotes from Nietzsche's works are cited by section or aphorism number, not by page number. I have referred to the Giorgio Colli – Mazzino Montinari edition (*Sämtliche Werke. Kritische Studienausgabe in 15 Bänden* [Berlin: de Gruyter, 1980]) for Nietzsche's work; the English translations I use are listed here. Occasionally, I have suggested alterations to the German translation.

The Antichrist (Der Antichrist), trans. R. J. Hollingdale (New York: Penguin Books, 1968).

Assorted Opinions and Maxims (Vermischte Meinungen und Sprüche), trans. R. J. Hollingdale (Cambridge: Cambridge University Press, 1986), vol. 2, pt. 1 of *Human, All Too Human*.

Beyond Good and Evil (Jenseits von Gut und Böse), trans. Walter Kaufmann (New York: Vintage Books, 1974).

The Birth of Tragedy (Der Geburt der Tragödie), trans. Walter Kaufmann (New York: Random House, 1967).

Daybreak (Morgenröte), trans. R. J. Hollingdale (Cambridge: Cambridge University Press, 1982).

Ecce Homo, trans. R. J. Hollingdale (New York: Penguin Books, 1979).

Friedrich Nietzsche on Rhetoric and Language, trans. S. Gilman, C. Blair, and D. Parent (Oxford: Oxford University Press, 1989).

On the Genealogy of Morals (Zur Genealogie der Moral), trans. Walter Kaufmann and R. J. Hollingdale (New York: Vintage Books, 1967).

The Gay Science (Die fröhliche Wissenschaft), trans. Walter Kaufmann (New York: Random House, 1974).

Human, All Too Human (Menschliches, Allzumenschliches), trans. R. J. Hollingdale (Cambridge: Cambridge University Press, 1986).

Truth and Philosophy: Selections from Nietzsche's Notebooks of the 1870's, trans. Daniel Breazeale (Atlantic Highlands, N.J.: Humanities Press), 1979.

Twilight of the Idols (Götzen-Dämmerung), trans. R. J. Hollingdale (New York: Penguin Books, 1968).

The Will to Power: Notes from the 1880's (Der Wille zur Macht), trans. Walter Kaufmann and R. J. Hollingdale (New York: Viking Press, 1968).

The Wanderer and His Shadow (*Der Wanderer und sein Schatten*), trans. R. J.
    Hollingdale (Cambridge: Cambridge University Press, 1986), vol. 2, pt. 2 of
    Human, All Too Human.
Thus Spake Zarathustra (*Also Sprach Zarathustra*), trans. R. J. Hollingdale (New
    York: Penguin Books, 1961).
Untimely Meditations (*Unzeitgemässe Betrachtungen*), trans. R. J. Hollingdale
    (Cambridge: Cambridge University Press, 1983).

A final word about the 'book that isn't', *The Will to Power*. As most readers of
Nietzsche in translation know, this work (the Hollingdale/Kaufmann translation)
is not, properly speaking, a book of Nietzsche's, but selections (variously arranged
and rearranged) from his notebooks. Clearly, any citations from these translated
bits of the *Nachlass* must be used judiciously, and I have included only those
passages from the 1880s that reinforce comparable material from the published
texts.

Approaching Nietzsche primarily through his published work may seem wholly
conventional, yet Heidegger's lectures on Nietzsche focus on the *Nachlass* and
give only secondary consideration to the texts published in Nietzsche's lifetime
(this in order to discover his so-called 'unthought'). I will leave the discussion of
this practice to Heidegger scholars; my criticisms of his Nietzsche lectures can be
found throughout.

Index